Lost Stitches

My great-grandfather Thomas Arnold Briggs,
founder of Bostitch

Lost Stitches

THE BOSTITCH LEGACY AND MY CRAZY JAMAICAN FAMILY

A retrospective

by

Daniel Archer Melville
with *Rachel Manley*

IAN RANDLE PUBLISHERS
Kingston • Miami

First published in Jamaica, 2020 by
Ian Randle Publishers
16 Herb McKenley Drive
Box 686
Kingston 6
www.ianrandlepublishers.com

National Library of Jamaica Cataloguing-In-Publication Data

Names: Melville, Daniel Archer, author.| Manley, Rachel,
    author.
Title: Lost stitches : the Bostitch legacy and my crazy Jamaican
    family : a retrospective / by Daniel Archer Melville with
    Rachel Manley.
Description: Kingston : Ian Randle Publishers, 2020.
Identifiers: ISBN 9789768286246 (pbk)
    ISBN 9789768286253 (hbk)|ISBN 9789768286260 (e-bk)
Subjects: LCSH: Melville, Daniel Archer – Family.
    |Briggs, Thomas Arnold, 1857-1928.|Briggs, Helen Ethelwyn,
    1879-1906.|Briggs, Berenice, 1890-1930|Melville, Harold Archer,
    1887-1951|Biography.|Genealogy.|Boston Wire Stitcher Company.
    |Bostitch Industrial Company.
Classification: DDC 920 -- dc23.

All photographs and images are from Danny Melville's personal
collection unless otherwise specified.

Cover and Book Design by Ian Randle Publishers
Printed and Bound in the United States of America

This book is dedicated to:

My wife Carole, my rock,
she endures my crazy gene.

My grandmother Berenice,
lost in the elusive mist of history.

My sons Marc, Alexander and Daniel,
the future, that they know their heritage.

Bostitch Factory 1904

Contents

Acknowledgements

Thank you to:

Jackie Ranston, for her indefatigable research on the Jamaican side of my family;

Nicholas Bornstein, Boston University, College of Arts and Sciences researcher for delving into the elusive history of my New England family;

Ainsley Henriques, keeper of Jewish history in Jamaica, for his knowledge and research.

Thanks also to:

Karl Watson in Barbados, Arnold Bertram in Jamaica and Cheryl Caruolo in Cambridge, Massachusetts for their help;

My Aunt Mary is the last of that generation; her amazing memory helped with fitting together invaluable pieces to this puzzle;

My cousins all, Tahiti Berenice and Perth Berenice on the Melville side; on the Lawrence side, Helen, Marianne and Dorothy for their memories, anecdotes, photos and encouragement to tell what is also their story. My Hastings cousins and my sister-in-law Angela Melville and my Uncle Richard Melville for invaluable photographs.

A special thanks to Pamela Melville McGregor who gave me some of the best insights and stories;

Antoinette 'Toni' Zitman, faithful friend of my mother's later years who shared their personal conversations;

Bonnie Munday, for her amazing help shaping and editing the story;

Deepto Chakrabarty, Professor of astronomy and nuclear physics at Massachusetts Institute of Technology (M.I.T.), a real Rocket Scientist and owner of Briggs Heritage House, 87 Medford St, Arlington, Massachusetts built by my great-grandfather Thomas Briggs in 1889, for opening his home to us and for sharing his own research of my family;

The late Wally Parks, whose appearance at Chukka Cove in 1993 started my journey and to his sister Lucille Iremonger whose biography, *Yes, My Darling Daughter*, gave me fierce insight into my paternal grandfather;

Israel Cinman who not only gave invaluable editorial insights but loaned Rachel Manley for the project;

Carole, my wife, for the beautiful restoration of the cover image of my grandmother and for the rehabilitation of the very old photographs for the book.

Finally, this book would have never been, but for Rachel, a lifelong friend, wordsmith, author, teacher. Rachel marvelled at the fact we didn't kill each other as we wrestled with this work over the past two years. I assured her there was still time.

Preface

If I included everything that took place in my life, this book would never end. And I couldn't include all the family; it is too large and extended, so where does one draw the line?

Almost all dates of travel are supported by ships manifests; births, deaths, all the important dates have been verified. The research in this story was extensive, but at times I have had to make some assumptions. Much of the information comes from interviews with the family; people often have different recollections of the same event, especially so within families, and at seventy-three I admit my memory is not what it used to be.

In the course of writing, I realized that Wally Parks who arrived at Chukka Cove that fateful day in 1993 – on a visit which in many ways started this journey, would be in his nineties if he were still alive. I went searching for him only to discover that he died in New Zealand in February 2020. It would have meant a lot to talk with him about what I had learned and to let him know that he was the one who planted the seed that took me on this incredible journey.

In piecing together this story of my family, I have deliberately refrained from trying to be politically correct, because as a Jamaican of another age, I never grew up that way and it would feel somewhat disingenuous to do otherwise. That's why I have tried to put into context those references to race the reader will find in the story, a subject whose subtleties one cannot ignore nowadays. I have often thought there is no louder way in which white privilege suggests itself than in the original 'one drop' rule that governed America's thinking on its big conundrum of race: that if a Caucasian had so much as that one drop of sub-Saharan or black blood, his or her racial assignation became black. This made me wonder why black and not white? In that American rule it is as though somehow the assumption is that one black drop tarnishes the whole. By that rationale, how come the drops of white blood don't tarnish the black?

The vast majority of Jamaicans are black. There are few if any pure white Jamaicans in my lifetime, but there are indeed Jamaicans who *think* they are white. In Jamaica colour is usually described as what you see. A brown person is exactly that, a brown person, beyond that there's a light or dark brown person. A Jamaican of fair complexion is sometimes referred to as a 'red-man', not because he's a descendant of a First Nation but because his skin turns red in the tropical sun! Our descriptions can be amusingly accurate, as we pinpoint the actual place in the range of the palette of a person's colour. And in a society whose motto "out of many one people" reflects a truly diverse population, these descriptions include the endless variety of mixtures that make up who we are.

I have described the people in my book as I have seen them, having in my heart the affection I bear for all humanity.

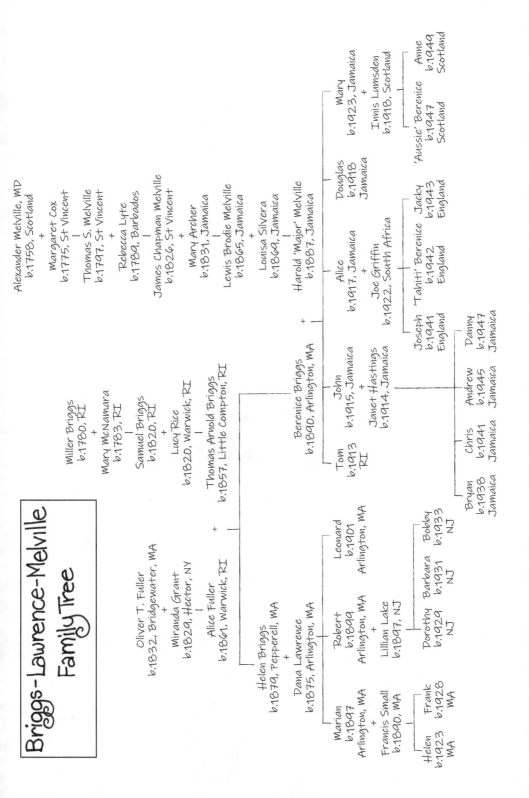

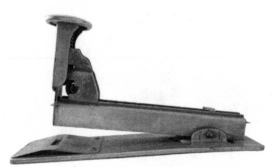

1924 Bostitch stapler

1

Arlington 2018

In the summer of 2018, I stood on the sidewalk in front of a house at 87 Medford Street in Arlington, Massachusetts, with my wife, Carole. It was a heritage house with a blue plaque on the wall. As houses go, it wasn't much to look at. An unimposing two-story building with two turrets, its grey stucco walls suggested a quiet austerity. It lay within a neatly trimmed, low hedge dominating a narrow plot of land. This house was built in 1889 by Thomas Arnold Briggs, inventor, industrialist, and multi-millionaire founder of Bostitch and my great-grandfather.

It had been the time of American ingenuity, invention, and industrial growth, and Thomas Briggs was an iconic name in these parts. In 1896 he had invented a machine that stitched books from a coil of wire. By 1900 the company had moved to East Greenwich, Rhode Island. The invention of the ingenious modern multi-staple machine that his company, The Boston Wire Stitcher Company (later shortened to Bostitch), began manufacturing for industrial and later office or personal use would become a household name in America and around the world.

I gazed at 'Briggs House' with its heritage plaque. It was near the road facing a cemetery, its entrance just a short flight of stone steps up, and it had a narrow verandah along the side. I walked up the steps and rang the bell. Professor Deepto Chakrabarty, a middle-aged Indian man who was an astronomer and nuclear physicist, opened the door, stepped outside, and closed it back carefully behind him. He greeted us but didn't invite us in; although he'd been expecting us he said he was anxious not to be too long as his young daughter was inside sleeping.

I had spoken to Mr Chakrabarty on the phone before I came to Boston, when I tracked down the house and its number. He was proud of having bought this heritage house, so much so that he had done his own research on the owner Thomas Briggs and seemed eager to share with me what information he had unearthed. I had told him that Thomas Briggs was my great-grandfather.

All my life I had been aware of my inventor great-grandfather as a shadowy figure. I considered his legend as distant and incomprehensible as most family stories of past glories and achievements. But I had always thought of him with curiosity, awe, and pride whenever I used a staple machine or held a book bound as it is by his technique, knowing these are the children of his imagination.

Mr Chakrabarty showed us briefly over the narrow grounds dominated by the house and we went around to the back where there stood a wide double garage whose door was rolled up to reveal an almost-empty cavernous interior.

"This is where so much happened," my host said pensively with a small gesture taking in the extent of the gloomy space we entered, which he explained he had renovated. At one side a ladder was suspended from a trapdoor, the mouth of a musty attic above, and I was curious about what might have been stored or concealed up there.

"I think this is where he invented the staple machine, the paper feeder, and the roller blind," explained Deepto. "The label machine was earlier. That seems to have started his career. And I believe the automatic gun device was invented later at the Division Street factory many years later, perhaps 1914 or 1915, for World War I."

I stood looking at the space to which my great-grandfather Thomas Briggs had retreated to don his thinking cap and work on his inventions, contrivances that in their own way had changed the way business offices everywhere worked, making them more efficient with equipment that we take for granted today.

I couldn't help but think back to the summer of 1958 when I was eleven and my brother Andrew and I accompanied our parents, John and Janet Melville, on a trip to the United States. We were going to see the new Bostitch plant in East Greenwich that had opened the previous year. In those days my mother refused to fly, so we sailed from Jamaica to Miami on the *Evangeline*, an old tub of a cruise ship that plied the Caribbean back then. It was my first trip overseas so there was much excitement, and it was a memorable one in many ways. We stayed two nights at the Colonial Hotel in Miami and took an overnight train to Boston in a Pullman coach. All kids love trains, and that ride was one of the highlights of the trip. We arrived at the station at Copley Square, loaded several suitcases into the cab and my father directed the driver to take us to the Copley Square Hotel – which was immediately across the road. The driver was not amused.

Opened in 1891, the hotel served as the face of Boston, a home-away-from-home for famous residents, visiting dignitaries, politicians, businessmen, and athletes. As a kid I was impressed by its elegance, a lot of plush carpets and polished brass. The elevators were manual, and I was delighted when the uniformed operator allowed me to try my hand on the lever.

The following day we took a short train ride to Providence, Rhode Island. We stayed at the Sheraton Biltmore Hotel, another landmark built in 1922. It was there I had my first prime rib, very rare, an inch thick, and covering the large plate. I'd never seen a piece of meat that big. We visited the Rhode Island Hospital Trust at 15 Westminster Street to meet with my father's financial advisor Phil Simons and his able assistant Dorothy Alker. To our family, Dorothy became the human face of The Rhode Island Hospital Trust; she became a friend and was invited to all the important family milestone celebrations. The Rhode Island Hospital Trust was founded in 1867 to manage the financial affairs of the Rhode Island Hospital. It became a significant local commercial bank where Thomas Briggs had established a trust for his sizeable estate for the benefit of his two daughters, Helen and Berenice. Berenice had married one Harold Melville and moved to his home country of Jamaica. They were to become my grandparents.

While my Dad tended to his business, we were given a tour of the bank. We were shown the vault and allowed to hold a US$1,000 note, about US$9,000 in today's dollars in one banknote! Eleven years later, the Nixon administration would pull those large notes from circulation in an early effort to curb criminality and money laundering. Another highlight of that 1958 trip was attending a concert of the Boston Pops Orchestra, conducted by the great Arthur Fiedler; my cousin Leonard, who was a supporter of the symphony, arranged the tickets.

The next day, we were taken to East Greenwich to the new Bostitch plant. There I met for the first time my father's first cousins Marian Lawrence Small, Robert Lawrence, and Leonard Lawrence, the children of my late great-aunt Helen Briggs-Lawrence and her husband Dana Lawrence. Along with my father and his siblings, they were the owners of 90 per cent of Bostitch through the Thomas Briggs trust. Dana had died eight years earlier in 1950. I met his second wife, Anna, then well into her eighties. When a few days later we went to visit the Lawrence family plot at the cemetery, I was surprised to see a plaque with Anna's name on it.

"But Aunt Anna isn't dead yet," I said in confusion to my mother. I can still hear them all laughing at me.

As an 11-year-old coming from a small island, I didn't know what to expect when I saw the plant. Pretty much the only factories I'd seen were the sugar factories on the large plantations that dotted the countryside in rural Jamaica. The Bostitch plant was the biggest building I had ever entered, and I was in awe as we toured the offices and factory, viewing the various pieces of equipment used to manufacture the staplers, nailing guns, and a host of other products Bostitch made. I realized this was just one of several plants and distribution centres the company operated globally. It was then that I first realized where the quarterly cheques that allowed us to live a privileged life in Jamaica came from. We were rich!

Growing up in rural Jamaica, a country of great poverty for many, I was aware that we were privileged, a comfortably well-off family, but it didn't seem to be something my parents made a big deal about. Though their lifestyle reflected relative wealth – my three older brothers and I attended private boarding schools – we never had pocket money like other kids. If we needed clothes, we just went to Issa or Hanna's department stores in Kingston, chose what we wanted, and signed on our father's account. I suppose you would call my father a country squire and gentleman farmer, and though he never worked a nine-to-five job, he was not at all a lazy man. He was always busy on his property while my mother tended her beloved gardens. We had a relatively large but modest, homey country house, and though we had many staff for our home and the property – to clean the pool and groom and care for the horses, to run the household – we had none of the ostentatious trappings of wealth of some of the richer families I knew who flaunted their stately homes, expensive status cars, and lavish lifestyles in Kingston. I didn't know then, but this modest characteristic in my parents actually reflected the natural reticence of established 'old' money.

Standing in Briggs's dim garage sixty years after that first childhood visit, I finally realized how my ancestor's labour and ingenuity had afforded three generations of Melvilles in Jamaica the comfortable lives we enjoyed. Many members of our family in Jamaica and beyond had lived as though our family's money would never end. And here in this musty unpretentious room was the source of much of our good fortune.

Our host brought out a framed photograph of Thomas Briggs and a list of previous owners of the house. But he was anxious to go back inside to his sleeping child. He promised to forward me all the research he had accumulated.

I considered the iconic plaque on the side of the house and couldn't help thinking of my own crazy family and the wider tribe of the Briggs line scattered over the globe, some eccentric, many depressed with tragic lives one way or another. So few had ever seriously tackled work or a career, and for the few who had, it hadn't always been plain sailing. But they always had that safety net that the hard work and innovation of my great-grandfather Briggs had afforded us all.

In the car going back to our hotel I found myself asking this question: how could it be that Berenice, the privileged youngest daughter of this wealthy American who had founded the great Bostitch Company, would leave a life of such social glamour and fame and style to marry a Jamaican named Harold Melville, and move to the colonial Caribbean in 1912?

Far from being today's tourist island whose white sand, blue seas, and palm fronds have attracted North Americans in droves, Jamaica was then a tough land to live in with its heat and mosquitoes, its social tensions and limited social life. I wondered why Berenice Briggs would opt for this relative obscurity and uncertainty, leaving the ease, respectability, and protection that her father's achievements would have ensured.

It turned out to be a question that wouldn't go away. I became determined to retrace the journey from Boston to Jamaica that produced my limb of the Briggs family. I had to find out what had enticed my grandmother to make such a bold move. My journey would lead me to learn a lot about Harold Melville, a mysterious figure nicknamed 'Major' about whom even my father, one of Harold's own sons, seldom talked. I wanted to know all I could find out about this iconic ancestor who had shaped the course of my family's life.

This would become my quest. And I was in for one interesting ride!

2

Ocho Rios 1993

In 1993, when I was forty-six, I was standing at the bar beside
the polo field at Chukka Cove Farm in St Ann parish, not
far from Ocho Rios. I remember it was a typically hot Jamaican
afternoon. We'd just finished playing polo and, soaking wet, I was
still in my britches and boots, having my usual Red Stripe beer
with a group of sweaty players, when an elderly gentleman I'd
never seen before walked over and introduced himself to me.

"I'm Wally Parks. You could say I'm an amateur genealogist."

Chukka Cove was not just a polo ground; it was my home. Ten
years earlier I had built six villas and kept the corner lot nearest the
sea for myself, giving my family over the years easy access to the
Caribbean Sea and to my great love, swimming. From the verandah
I could look out to a sea of contradictory colours, a puzzle of rainbow
patches. Down a gentle slope the cove had a small white sand beach
and wading pool where children loved to play and where adults
could relax. But to swim one had to pick one's way across the sharp
limestone rocks, with cavities like lace from centuries of salty
erosion, and dive off the cliff. I would swim beyond the small inlet

of white sand, further along the rugged coast, into a cave we called Bat Cave where, as one enters, thousands of bats dart in calamitous motion, and where below the purest turquoise water, gem-like with faceted brilliance as it shifts and sloshes, lays the whitest sand I have ever seen anywhere. Inside that cave I always felt somehow special, as though I was sharing in some quiet secret of the universe. Scenes from the famous movie *Papillon*, starring Hollywood icons Steve McQueen and Dustin Hoffman, were filmed there in the early 1970s, some years before I purchased the land.

I created a polo ground, equestrian and trail riding facility. I designed it all on this naturally beautiful spot and have been told it is one of the loveliest polo grounds in the world. Its unique coastal setting has hosted several international events and polo tournaments. We held clinics with world-class equestrian trainers and coaches like Captain Mark Phillips and Jack Le Goff, the coach of the US Olympic three-day event team. Some of the best polo players in the world have played at Chukka, all the while improving the level of our local polo players; we did the same with visiting equestrian riders and coaches. We even attempted group horseback-riding holidays. Guests would ride up through the hills of St Ann for two nights and back down to swim in the sea at Chukka.

Anyone familiar with the sport knows that polo and equestrian pursuits don't easily make money. Eventually, in the mid-1990s when I was going slowly broke, we introduced trail riding for a mass market from local hotels and cruise lines, and this was how our now very successful business, Chukka Caribbean Adventures, began. We even pioneered swimming horses as a tour, which is still popular today after thirty-six years. But the day that Wally Parks walked into my life in 1993, I was still struggling to make the business work; that's what was preoccupying my mind.

Wally Parks, a Jamaican who had emigrated to New Zealand many years before, was probably then in his mid-60s. I'd never met him before, but he seemed to know me and proceeded to tell me an incredible and bewildering story about my paternal grandfather, Harold Melville.

"My sister, Lucille Iremonger," he explained, "wrote a book in 1964, and she put a chapter in it about your grandfather."

We talked for hours. *Yes, My Darling Daughter* was a memoir based on Lucille's childhood growing up in Jamaica in the 1920s and '30s. One of the chapters was called 'The Major'. Wally explained that the chapter was about my grandfather, Major Harold Melville. Wally and his sisters knew him well when they were children; indeed, their family had for a while been overwhelmed by the Major's presence in their lives. That's because, after his first wife, my grandmother Berenice, died, Major was lonely and needed help with his five motherless children. So he had sought the company of their mother, Ivy Parks, a married woman with a family.

Grandfather Melville had died in 1951, when I was four years old. I only vaguely remember meeting him once or twice. To me he was always just a distant and incomprehensible figure, as most parents' stories of people who were their elders or even contemporaries are to children, even when they are family. But Wally was in his mid-20s when Harold died, and so he remembered the Major well. He talked about 'The Major' with a certain affection, mentioning his interests, which included horseracing, bird shooting, cockfighting, and women, not in that order. This wasn't my first inkling of my grandfather's penchant for the fairer sex. I already knew about three 'outside' children who were my uncles; I had met two of them. They were all born during the time Major was married to my grandmother, Berenice, so nothing I heard about his peccadillos really surprised me, including this revelation from

Wally. I guess the Major was what most Jamaicans call with mischievous reverence a 'cocksman'. Jamaican macho men have been promiscuous for countless generations, so this in itself was not remarkable, then or now. We weren't the only family, privileged or not, with similar stories of infidelity.

It was becoming clear to me that Wally had known Grandfather Melville quite well, and while I knew about some of what Wally shared that afternoon, I knew nothing about most of this family lore. While I was growing up my father, John, never spoke much about his family – not of his father, Harold, his younger brother Douglas who was killed in the Second World War, nor of his older brother Thomas, Tom, who 'lost it' and was put in an asylum. And he never spoke at all about his mother, Berenice. He didn't talk about his famous grandfather Thomas Briggs either, though in fact Briggs had visited Jamaica a few times, the last being in 1927, the year before he died. My dad was then twelve years old and would certainly have remembered him. To this day, I wonder why he never spoke of any of them.

My father grew up riding and competing at gymkhana events at Knutsford Park racetrack in Kingston. He was an excellent horseman and won several races as an amateur jockey on his beloved gelding *Gibraltar*. He learned a lot about horses from Major's cousin, racehorse trainer Owen Silvera, who had lived for a time with the family. Eventually, my dad gravitated to polo and played that noble sport until old injuries forced his retirement. In truth, he lost interest shortly after my older brother, Chris, the second born (I was the fourth and last), had a terrible accident playing a tournament, ending up in a coma for a month and keeping him in hospital for several more months. My mother visited him every single day and nagged my father to quit polo.

The little I knew about my grandfather Harold was that he was born in Jamaica and his own mother Louisa had died when he was very young. He himself got very sick with rheumatic fever as a child. Harold didn't get on with his father's second wife, and it was left to his mother's sister, Luna, to look after him. Perhaps to make up for his sense of loss and vulnerability, Harold took up boxing to build up and defend himself, and took daily long walks, the start of a lifelong love of sport and outdoor life.

A rare story about his father told by my dad is of a neighbour who had come to the house to complain that he had heard each of Major's twenty or more Spanish game-fighting cocks crowing that particular morning. Major solved that complaint by turning to his main man and telling him to bring a few more fighting cocks in from the farm in St Thomas. The neighbour never returned to complain again.

I had always known that Major loved shooting, shotguns for dove hunting, skeet and trap shooting, as well as pistols and rifles for target shooting, and that he taught my dad to shoot at a very early age. My dad in turn made shooting his lifelong passion, travelling over the years to Mexico, Nicaragua, El Salvador, and parts of South America to hunt ducks and doves, and to Saskatchewan for Canada geese. He lived for shooting. He was on the Jamaica skeet shooting team for the 9th Central American and Caribbean Games in 1962, the year of Jamaica's Independence.

As Wally chatted on, I became aware how fond he was of my late grandfather. I was utterly absorbed by everything he shared about him and the wider Melville family tribe. Wally soon launched into a long and involved account of the Melville family tree, which seemed to stretch from Scotland in 1066 all the way to modern-day St Vincent and even Guyana. He promised to provide me with more information on the Melvilles from ancient to modern times, including the fact that the British Broadcasting Corporation (BBC) naturalist, David Attenborough, had made reference to a book in which there was mention of an H.P.C. Melville on the north coast of South America. It was all news to me, though of course I knew ours was an old Scottish family, a clan with its own tartan and coat of arms featuring dogs that I had seen. And whenever I'd think of ancient men in tartan kilts blowing bagpipes, I wondered like most of the rest of the world what rescued their swinging nuts from curious onlookers and the cold northern wind.

"He arrived in Guyana at an early age and married *two* Indian women – definitely a Melville!" Wally said highly amused, speaking about some ancient ancestor (I wasn't really following the list of names at that stage). We laughed about that though I wasn't quite sure then why that was typical of a Melville. My own father, a quiet man, had been a devoted husband and steady presence as a father. My brothers and I, far from being notable studs, had suffered our fair share of rejections growing up. As for me, I first married Winsome with whom I had three sons. We divorced and later on after a second marriage failed, I married Carole, my current wife.

Wally and I talked for hours that afternoon and consumed several beers. When the sun began casting a sideways glance of orange light in a reflection on the nearby water, Wally said he wanted to leave before it got dark, but promised that he'd send me some old photographs of my grandfather and a photocopy of 'The Major' chapter from his sister's book. I would later discover that Lucille Iremonger had, in fact, published several books, won Jamaica's prestigious Musgrave Medal for literature and had been the literary critic of *The London Sunday Telegraph*.

"Don't forget to read that chapter," Wally reminded me as he shook my hand. "You'll get to know your grandfather. You see, he was having an affair with my mother." The air went still between us. "My sister explains it all in her book."

"I won't forget," I assured him. That had whetted my appetite. How could it not? Later, I would discover that every word Wally told me that afternoon about both Major Melville and the wider clan would prove to be true. Little did I know that this visit would one day dovetail into my own search for the past, providing important clues to help me find both sides of my family.

I have often wondered what possessed Wally to seek me out and share with me a painful story of his mother's affair with my grandfather. It must be because it was something he didn't want to forget.

3

My Parents

here are many variations of a very old saying that goes something like this: *If a person is not a liberal by age 20 he has no heart; if he's not a conservative by 40, he has no head.* If that adage is true, then I still have no head at seventy-three! I no longer consider myself a rebel or a radical, but I'm socially conscious, colour-blind, I believe in human rights, and that love is love. I believe in science, that climate change is real, that education and universal health care are rights not privileges, and most other liberal causes.

I share this here to place myself in relation to my country and my family's stories. I'd like you, the reader, to know something about who I am personally, socially, and politically. I think it's important to know who an author is and to be aware of the perspective from which the story is being told. As I look back on the youth that really provided the loam for the person I would grow to be, there are many gaps about things I feel I should have known or noticed at the time but didn't. Perhaps most kids are just busy growing up, bent on their own missions so that by the time you think to ask, your parents are gone. So in assembling this chapter I was helped very much by my wife Carole, who is more observant then I am, and by Toni Zitman, a loyal and trusted friend of my mother in later years. I should mention here that we boys grew up calling our parents, Janet and John, 'Ma' and 'Pops', and our friends did likewise. Ma shared many secrets with Toni whose generous retelling of them to me helped draw the picture I have of my mother and her life that were out of reach of my memory.

My parents were basically conservative in outlook, not in an aggressive or ideological kind of way but were typical of people who are comfortable and to whom life had been kind and who want things to remain the way they are. Why change what is working? With my Dad's inheritance, everything ticked like clockwork. My dad was happy pottering about the farm, being around his horses and with his shooting while my mother loved her garden and her gin and tonics fondly known as G&Ts. Along with us four boys, they seemed satisfied with life. I didn't really know everything that went on behind those G&Ts, but one got the sense that it was quite naturally a close and loving marriage. They seemed to have an unspoken but instinctive understanding of each other. Like all marriages I'm sure they had their issues, but I never heard them quarrel. My father affectionately called my mother 'Muzzie', and for as long as I can remember, he would serve his Muzzie breakfast in bed every morning. I can't help wondering if his chivalrous consideration of our mother may have stemmed from a determination not to treat her the way he had seen Major treat his mother.

They had married in February 1937, after having met when Janet, née Hastings, was on a walk and John rode by on a horse. Toni says the walk wasn't just chance; Ma had admitted she took those walks having set her sights on an attractive and eligible man on his aristocratic horse. My dad's sister, Aunt Mary, also confided in Toni that the family considered Janet a gold-digger. I'm not sure what that meant in those days; back then, what else was a woman brought up to do but marry well? I don't know if the horse was white, and certainly my dad was not a heroic prince, but I like to think that John rescued my mother from a financially uncertain fate in Jamaica just as she probably rescued him from the echoes of an insecure youth.

The Melvilles, Lawrences and the Briggs are the focus of this book, but my mother has an interesting family story too, one of the widely varied strands that make up Jamaica. And believe me, there is no Jamaican story that doesn't involve the question of colour.

Janet Mima Hastings was born in Kingston, Jamaica, on March 22, 1914, a few months before the start of the First World War. Her mother, Vida Jones, a brown lady, was the daughter of a postmistress and a shopkeeper from the parish of Portland. Janet's father, Norman Hastings, was a white Englishman from an aristocratic family whose father was a physician. The family of six lived at 13 Queen Anne Street, Cavendish Square, Marylebone, London, with almost as many staff comprising a nurse, a cook, and three housemaids. Norman boarded at Uppington School on High Street in the quaint town of Uppington, Rutland County, England. Founded in 1584, Uppington School is to this day one of the top English boarding schools.

According to Ma, her father went to Florida for a citrus business venture that failed because of a terrible freeze. Indeed, The Great Freeze of 1894-95 ruined most of the groves in Florida and citrus production fell from five million boxes a year in 1893 to a mere 147,000 boxes in 1895. Norman would have been twenty-nine years old in 1894 and probably lost every penny he had on the venture. He then came to Jamaica and worked with the United Fruit Company, an American corporation that grew and exported bananas from several Caribbean islands and Central America to the US. It could be that Norman didn't want to return to England a failure or he may have been the black sheep of the family. In those days it was not uncommon for aristocratic British families to export their problem sons to the colonies.

It's not clear when Norman arrived in Jamaica from the US or when he met Vida, but we do know they were married in Kingston on March 21, 1912. He was twenty-three years older than her, and they would have five children – the first born in August that same year. My mother Janet was their second child.

To understand why Vida, a pretty 23-year-old light brown-skinned Jamaican girl, would marry an Englishman twenty-three years her senior, you would have to understand colour and class in the colonial Jamaican society. During the period of slavery, the English plantation owners and their Irish, Scottish, and Welsh bookkeepers and overseers bred frequently with enslaved women creating a large pool of what were known as free coloureds, half-caste mulattoes. In case you believe that the English plantation owners, their white overseers and bookkeepers were not enjoying plantation life, it's worth considering an estimate of Jamaica's population in 1834, the year of Emancipation, provided by the historian Arnold Bertram, in which the data showed there were 16,600 whites, 31,300 free coloured, 11,000 free blacks, and 311,000 enslaved Africans and people of African descent. Bertram states,

How do we explain this seemingly contradictory development? Whereas the growth of the black population was the result of the forced transportation of some 700,000 enslaved Africans to the island to provide labour for the plantation economy, the coloured population came into existence as the progeny of enslaved African women and white British colonists.

White men back then considered blacks to be sub-human but they were quite happy to use enslaved females whom they found irresistible as comfort women. Matthew Gregory 'Monk' Lewis, the famous English novelist and dramatist, whose family owned plantations in Jamaica wrote, "Beautiful are their forms in general, and easy and graceful are their movements which indeed appear to me so striking that they cannot fail to excite the admiration of anyone." That sounds like lust to me. The attraction extended all the way to the top of British officialdom on the island. The Duke of Manchester, a governor of Jamaica, was 'a begetter of numerous brown-skinned illegitimate progeny'; one estimate put the figure at sixteen illegitimate children.

The British had a unique system to restore the population to full 'whiteness'. There were several stages; if a mulatto girl had a child with a white man, that child would have been called a quadroon (three-quarters white and one-quarter black). A quadroon girl and a white man produced an octoroon – one-eighth black and seven-eighths white – while the next cross was a hexadecaroon, or one-sixteenth black, fifteen-sixteenths white. And the next cross? Presto! White again. Thus, it would have been desirable in society at the time for Vida to marry Norman, as somewhere down the line the hope was they'd eventually get someone who looked white. Well, they got me!

It seemed one could say anything back then and it was okay; for example, when I was growing up there was a disgusting verse that went like this: 'If yu white yu alright, if yu brown yu can stick around, but if yu black go back.' The sad thing is that it was absolutely true. In colonial Jamaica, the lighter your skin colour the better your chances of upward mobility.

One can see why some Jamaicans in the years after the abolition of slavery sought to 'improve' their status and chances of success in life by increasing their 'whiteness'. So while many educated middle-class black women remained spinsters, well-to-do black Jamaican men would seek and marry lighter-skinned women in the certain knowledge the children would be more easily accepted. More recently, Jamaica has adopted the term 'browning' for a brown-skinned woman. Jamaican reggae icon Buju Banton says it clearly in his 1992 hit, *Love Me Browning*: "...me love me car me love me bike me love me money and ting, but most of all me love me Browning."

I feel the need to point out here that the Americans had an even more racist system of hypodescent, or ethnic designation, which was referred to as the one-drop rule. It was a social and legal principle of racial classification that was historically prominent in the US as recently as in the twentieth century. It asserted that any person with even one ancestor of sub-Saharan African ancestry ('one drop' of 'black' blood) is considered black (Negro or coloured in historical terms).

Well, fuck me, how dumb were these people? I'm proud of my drops.

Toni shared an interesting perspective on Ma growing up. She suggested that Ma's mother, Vida, had been brought up to be 'a proper lady' by her parents, a pastor and his postmistress wife, and that therefore Vida in turn was probably a strict mother to her girls, Alice and Janet. Although one would definitely call my mother 'a proper lady', I am not aware of any of this. I suppose Vida's shopkeeper dad might have been a deacon as well, but more likely they were just a good Christian family in Portland.

Alice would have been a cooperative child, but Ma, born the attention-getting drama queen of the family, ("Miss, watch me, watch me," according to Toni), would have been the defiant one. "While her mother corrected her, her father probably smiled at her antics. A little girl would love anyone who takes kind notice of them personally."

Sadly, Norman suffered from depression and eventually took to the bottle. Toni reminded me that while Norman might have been a boozer, he was probably just a pleasant happy degenerate alcoholic and not a violent loudmouth – a weak man – which wouldn't have mattered at all to little Janet. So Ma hardly mentioned her mother other than her punishments, but adored her father and always had good memories of him. She craved his attention. Toni got the impression that Ma misbehaved to be noticed and would invariably end up being punished by her mother for some infraction. My mother, whom Toni knew to be wilful to the day she died, seemed to be a handful even as a child.

Norman died on April 16, 1921, in Kingston. The death certificate gave the cause of death: "a) Chronic Alcoholism, b) Cardiac Failure." He was fifty-six years old. Janet was only seven and she'd lost her special ally, the one who understood her mischief. Three years later, in August 1924, Vida set off with her five children in tow for Avonmouth, England, aboard the *Coronado*. Norman's two spinster sisters, my great-aunts Alice 'Polly' and Mabel 'Mabs' had embraced their brother's widow and her five children and brought them to England to live so the children could attend boarding school. It was an act of kindness that then would have cost a fair bit of change, I'm sure.

I remember Ma telling a tale of getting boiled cabbage for the fifth time in a week at boarding school and counting nine little snails which she displayed around the edge of her plate. I believe Aunt Polly was the disciplinarian as we didn't hear much about her while my mother spoke fondly about Aunt Mabs, the younger sister, who was a quite well-known artist. My mother appears to have had an entirely self-interested approach to judging people she knew: it was strictly on the basis of how they suited her needs. This approach would persist to the end of her days.

Aunt Mabs mostly painted animal portraits – cats, dogs, and horses – and her work, always signed M.H., can still be found in antique art galleries in England. She gave a pastel landscape dated 1936 to Ma, who cherished that work of art until she died. It hangs on my wall today.

Toni thought that Aunt Polly must have been a proper gentrified middle-aged Victorian spinster. Ma described how during the holiday from boarding school, the aunts would have them come to stay one at a time: "The chauffeur would come and take her to Polly (who wasn't touchy-feely). You went into the room and you stood at the edge of the carpet, no further, and you got your welcome speech." Toni got the impression Aunt Polly didn't fully approve of Janet; it was Mabs who befriended Janet. On one of these visits, when my mother might have been around fourteen or fifteen, she was taken to the theatre. She was so excited; she even got a new dress and new shoes. She loved the theatre and maybe this excursion inspired her desire to try acting.

Says Toni, "Polly took her to an afternoon tea party at some lady's house who was a great friend of Charles Dickens, and she said Dickens always gave this lady his new manuscripts to read. He never printed anything unless this lady approved, she said. But it seems to me that she may have been embroidering this part of the story!"

Being exposed at an impressionable age to an exciting life of artists, writers, and painters would appeal to a young Jamaican girl. Maybe this was where her tendency to narcissism and dreams of becoming a theatre star began. Even though Ma told us the boarding school served boiled cabbage too often, she treasured a little medal she had won for elocution. At around age seventeen, after she graduated, armed with her medal and an excellent letter of recommendation, she went to London for an audition at Polly's suggestion. She was hoping to pursue a career in the theatre – but was told she was too short and too dark!

This was incredibly hurtful and probably scarred her for life the way these things do. She never shared it with me until a few months before she died. "I don't think it was Ma's colour," said Toni, "She would have been mildly brown, like an Italian or Mediterranean girl. I think she might have been too full of herself or tried too hard and bombed on a word in the script that she misread. I think Mabs might have paid to have her enrolled in Italia Conte for elocution and dance classes. She says that she 'taught elocution and dance' at the school, but I'm sure that was a fairy story. 'Look it up,' she would insist. 'Quite a few famous actresses today were trained there!'"

Look it up, my mother had said. And in that phrase was a profound message. This dream of Ma's that seventy years later she shared with Toni was real. Italia Conti is still real in the world, and it was still real to Ma. It has always been a feather in Ma's cap that she attended the Academy. I looked it up:

The Italia Conti Academy is a performing arts educational institution based in London, England, delivering a variety of disciplines and theatre training at Secondary Education, Further Education and Higher Education. It was founded in 1911 by the actress Italia Conti.

Eight years after going to England, my mum reluctantly returned to Jamaica in October 1932 at eighteen years old with her mother, her older sister Alice, and a younger brother, Teddy. The other two brothers remained in England, one studying medicine, the other enrolled in the army. It was time, and Janet really had no choice as I don't think Mabs or Polly wanted the responsibility of an 18-year old. On returning, Vida probably had some money. She had received her husband's share when Polly and Mabs sold the family property, but Ma had to find herself a job, and she chose to be a schoolteacher, of all things. I don't know which parish she chose to work in or what she was hired to teach, but Toni tells me the first job lasted about a week. Her second teaching foray was in a school run by nuns! Toni asked her what she was supposed to teach and she said English. I'm not sure Ma even knew what a curriculum looked like. According to Toni she lasted one whole day before being fired by the head nun. I am not surprised – I just can't imagine my atheist, rebellious, maverick mother working with nuns.

I believe that after this inauspicious start, she decided to check out the marriage market. Janet confided in Toni that she'd watch Pops riding his horse on Hagley Park Road where they both happened to live and decided to start going out for walks. That apparently did the trick. One day, he stopped the horse and spoke to her and from there, says Toni, "you have the start of the John Melville family dynasty."

Toni said that Aunt Mary, John's sister, told her that they were upset with John because they all thought she was a 'gold-digger', and Major probably detested her because it is said he disliked Vida, probably because she was brown-skinned. For her part, Ma didn't talk about her in-laws, but Toni didn't think Janet cared much for my dad's sister. Conversations were always overly polite, and I couldn't help thinking that if Mary actually referred to my mother as a gold-digger, she really couldn't have been a friend!

Toni heard that Ma got married in Major's living room. "Ma must have been desperate to marry John…any which way she could have him...because she gave up the church wedding and the bridal gown and the glorious walk down the aisle, which was probably one of her biggest dreams."

They spent their honeymoon in England. Toni remarked wryly that Ma made sure she took John to England to shove him up her snobby Aunt Polly's nose. After an extended trip they returned home to a married life, one that I remember as a tight-knit family unit. I wasn't aware of grandparents, either Hastings or Melvilles. My mother never really spoke of Major. All I knew of him when I was growing up was that eight years after my father's mother died, Major got married to a much younger woman.

Toni's description of Ma's life with my father rings true – John indulging her by always having her dressed to 'puss backfoot' – a Jamaican saying meaning being kept in the latest fashions. "She was *someone*," Toni said as though the pride was all her. "She was Mrs John Melville!"

But Toni didn't think this garnered her many friends. She told me my mother once attended a wedding, beautifully dressed, and the next day the newspapers had Mrs John Melville's photographs and a description of her spectacular outfit, "...and bugger all about the bride whose wedding Ma was quite happy to upstage." Sounds like Ma!

On another occasion, Ma told Toni that Pops had a ball gown made for her with 400 *yards* of French lace. "Now that story was a big whopper. I don't think Pops was rich enough to purchase that amount of French lace. So it was a dress with *some* French lace. Ma could never walk dressed in that amount of lace, especially after a few drinks; it would be too heavy." This made me laugh. The exaggeration was so like my mother! I also learned that apparently my mother couldn't bring herself to attend her mother's funeral;

according to Toni, my father had said at the time funerals upset her too much.

"Putting aside her vanity, selfishness, and narcissism, Ma did have many good points. She liked to garden; she cared for her indoor plants; she arranged flowers beautifully; and she could knit from socks to Afghans. She enjoyed people visiting as long as no one talked about God. She was generous to her maid Lisa and the workers in the senior residences. At Christmas she always had a long list of gifts to buy for the caregivers and their children. Whenever I took her shopping she would always check to see if there was anything I would like her to get for me."

I thought about what I could say were Ma's characteristics good or bad, from the perspective of her son, and could only come up with the fact that she was a stickler for good manners and etiquette, something she tried her best to drill into her four sons. The dining table had to be set just so, and you were called out if you didn't use the silverware correctly or spoke with food in your mouth. As for my mother's personality, perhaps that's a hard thing for a son to describe; maybe when one has grown up with and lived close to a person for so many years it is difficult to extract the essences, to separate and pull out what is long buried in one's head in a single impression of what one knows. Little of what Toni said other than the factual details was new to me, but I couldn't have drawn that image myself. So, to paint an even clearer picture, I recently asked Carole how she'd describe her.

My wife is an artist – a painter. She paints excruciatingly accurate portraits that capture likenesses not just physical but of a person's spirit. She paints in the punctilious style of the French painter George Seurat. So one can say she has a discerning eye. She sees, and she sees through. Yet to the outside world, she is like a privet hedge, a dense and complicated arrangement of perfect leaves that creates a wall that no one can see through; only she can look out at the world as it passes by. Carole is not a big talker, but that afternoon she sent me her description in an email.

Ma:

Vain, Preoccupied with beauty

Showed disdain for overweight women

Always watched her figure/weight

Prided herself on having very narrow feet

Lisa her "maid" worked for the family for many years and worked for her five days a week when she went into the nursing home, until the very end.

Wore makeup every day to almost her last day...towards the end Lisa would apply the makeup for her

Always had her nails and toes painted but prided herself in painting them herself

Self-centered

Fastidious

Impressed with aristocracy

Loved the royal family

Proper and pretentious lifestyle was very important to her

Kind-hearted and generous

Did not understand money and would spend huge amounts on fresh flowers, clothes and shoes while John was alive; even to the end she always had fresh cut flowers brought to her room.

Perfect hearing and almost perfect eyesight to the end

Knitted every day

Avid reader

Enjoyed old classic movies

Drank a huge martini every afternoon for years

Went on to drink one glass of "Stoneleigh" Sauvignon Blanc every afternoon for her last 15 years

Would not accept any age-related deterioration, always said "something must be done"

Not a large eater, avoided carbs and ate everything "low fat" BUT loved KFC chicken and Spam

There she was. My mother! Carole had sketched her for me. I recognized every trait, every detail, every cell of my mother in that description.

The partnership between my parents lasted fifty-five years, until my Dad passed away suddenly in 1992. Janet, my Mum was a survivor. In the mid -1960s when she was about fifty years old, she underwent emergency surgery in Kingston to remove a tumour in her colon. The surgery was a success and I remember being shown the tumour which was the size of a large grapefruit. The surgery had saved her life but there was no guarantee the cancer would not reoccur, and it did. After only three months the doctors confirmed the worst and advised that a second surgery was not an option. My dad turned to his New England family who arranged for Ma to see a specialist in Boston. It was a sombre moment as my brothers and I bade them farewell at the airport as we were not sure if we would ever see her again. After a battery of consultations and tests Ma was given a long course of chemotherapy and after a few weeks my parents returned to Jamaica where she continued the chemo regime at home at Arthur's Seat. We were told her hair would fall out but it didn't and eventually the cancer disappeared. She made a full recovery and lived for another fifty years. Ma had smoked like a chimney but quit after the cancer ordeal. However, she drank up to the day before she died at one hundred years and seven months in October, 2014. I don't know if my mother was a happy woman nor can I tell if my father was. I think he was happy with my mother, and I think my mother felt safe with him. Maybe they felt safe with each other, those were not the days when parents shared their business with their children, but days when you married for life.

4

Jamaican Through and Through

Now I'll tell you why much of what I did as a kid growing up would have horrified my parents if they'd known. The first time I smoked ganja was at my family home, 'Arthur's Seat', in rural St Ann on the north coast of Jamaica. It happened in what we called the bottom garden – not my mom's fancy garden surrounding the house – and I was about fourteen. In the school holidays when we were not riding horses, I would hang out with the workers on the farm or the gardeners who tended my mother's large flower and vegetable garden. Ephraim Henry, the senior gardener, used to smoke 'jackass rope' made of locally grown tobacco that was rolled into a rope and sold in the rural farmers' markets by the foot. You would then unravel a bit of the 'rope', pick the best leaf to use as a wrapper, and roll short strips of tobacco leaf into a stubby cigar. Ephraim used to mix a little ganja in with his tobacco, so I inveigled him to let me try some of his 'jackass rope' as I wanted to experience ganja.

Back in the 1960s Jamaica's sativa strains of marijuana were mild compared to the high THC hybrids of today. I don't remember getting high from the weed, but I do remember getting very sick from the strong tobacco and I puked my heart out.

I had bad dyslexia and probably attention-deficit disorder before anyone even knew what those words meant. There was no remedial programme in Jamaica back then, no help to be had, no extra time to do exams. At best you were considered a slow learner; at worst just plain stupid or even more unkindly, a dunce.

I was the youngest of four boys in my family, and my father would regularly confuse our names. He solved the problem by referring to us by number and adding son. Me being the youngest, dad called me, 'Number 4 Son'. When I think about it, it's likely that my dad was probably dyslexic himself. For a fact, he had no college education (but as one of the beneficiaries of the Briggs fortune did he even need one?).

My brothers and I were sent to boarding school when we were very young. Andrew, the third born, and I attended prep school in Mandeville, Manchester, and then a series of high schools, first the prestigious Munro College in St Elizabeth, from which Chris – the second eldest – along with five other students who had just passed their final exams were expelled by the born-again Christian headmaster for celebrating their scholastic achievement with a couple beers. My father got into a rage and yanked us out of there.

It was then decided that Andrew and I would be sent to some high-priced private boarding school in New England where my father kept his money; in the meantime we spent a year at York Castle high school in Brown's Town, St Ann. The plan to go to the US never materialized, and the following year we were sent to another equally notable educational establishment, Jamaica

College (JC) in Kingston. It was 1961 and since this was my third high school in as many years, it probably didn't do much to help me overcome what was clearly my learning disability. JC was one of the oldest boys' boarding schools on the island founded with an endowment from a repentant slave-owning Englishman, Charles Drax, and it was exciting for me, a country boy, to be in the big city.

I was fifteen in 1962, the year of Jamaica's independence from Britain when things began to change; all Jamaicans had high expectations of prosperity and a bright future for our island. For me the most memorable image was the lowering of the Union Jack, and the raising of the Jamaican flag – black, green, and gold. In our family we never even thought of keeping our British passports, happy to have these exchanged for Jamaican ones. After all, Jamaica's future looked rosy; we had no debt, growth between 1950 and 1955 was at the rate of 10 per cent and steadily growing; we were being compared to the success story of the city-state of Singapore at the time.

Although I was never musical, it is interesting that music has sporadically played such an important role in shaping my life. Around the time of Independence, the Jamaican genres of ska and rock steady (reggae came some years later), that were coming out of Kingston's ghettos were popular with the downtown people but didn't get much airplay on Jamaica's two radio stations, which back then broadcast news, general programmes, English soap operas, and music that was confined almost exclusively to American and British rock and pop.

Three decades later I was to show tangible support for the *real* Jamaican music by becoming a foundation shareholder in Jamaica's and the world's first all-reggae radio station, aptly named *IRIE* FM. But in the days that I was at boarding school, we boys were desperate to hear this music – so we'd break out at night to visit the dance halls, leaving pillows stuffed under our bedsheets as a decoy. You see, sound systems – a turntable playing local music through giant, throbbing speakers set up in yards, villages, or town squares – had been around for years and were a big part of Jamaican music culture. In the '60s they became more sophisticated and louder, playing bass frequencies at 30,000 watts and more. The two leading operators of the day, Clement Dodd and Duke Reid, developed a rivalry, and to fill the dance halls they needed new and exclusive music. This led the two to go into music production of singles known as 'dubplates' exclusively for their own sound systems. And so it was that in an attempt to replicate American R&B, local musicians had created a uniquely Jamaican genre, Ska. We had to hear this stuff; hence our sneaky trips to those dance halls.

In boarding school, we slept on bunk beds in a dormitory with maybe twenty or thirty students with communal showers and toilets. This was a melting pot of teenagers from all walks of life; bright boys from poor families who had won government scholarships dumb rich kids whose parents could afford it, and everyone in between.

Around that time, I met Rachel Manley, a dear friend to this day. Rachel is the granddaughter of Jamaican National Hero Norman Manley, a brilliant Rhodes scholar, and a veteran of the First World War. On his return to Jamaica after the war he founded the People's National Party (PNP), Jamaica's first modern political movement in the 1930s and a model for many of the emerging political parties in the English-speaking Caribbean in that nationalistic era for the region.

During my teenage years, Rachel, Carole, and I would often visit the Manley's mountain retreat at Mavis Bank, deep in the Blue

Mountains. It was unfathomable to me driving the narrow winding country roads that anyone could have even found this spot. There on this beautiful, quite improbably isolated hilltop, Norman had built a log cabin where he planted coffee and ortaniques, a unique variety of citrus, and would walk the property, build rough furniture in the out-hut he used as a workshop, and no doubt have private time to read and see his family.

I was in awe of Norman Manley. He would sit and talk to us youngsters about Jamaica in ways I had never thought about my country before – it's history, his dreams for its destiny. Here was a man who had been Jamaica's most successful lawyer who cared not a jot about material things and who talked about our colonial history and embraced the concept of an independent destiny and culture for the black masses who though paramount to him, seemed almost inconsequential in the minds and concerns of the adults amongst whom I grew up. We called Norman 'Pardi'; we would follow him along his hillside walks among ferns and mossy paths under the pine trees, and end up sitting on a bench strategically placed to capture the view, where he'd stop to expound further on his themes on Jamaica. He was the first person to awaken a social conscience in me. Although my instincts had always drawn me to the company of simple country folk, now I was learning about their brutal history and being shown a vision of their possibilities.

Back then Norman's younger son, Michael, Rachel's father, was the Island Supervisor of the PNP-affiliated National Workers Union (NWU). He would later be voted in to lead the party his father founded, and in 1972 became Jamaica's fourth prime minister.

Between like-minded students whom I befriended at Jamaica College and the liberal, some would say leftist, views of the Manley household, which I visited often, what choice did I have but to become an angry young man? This was the 1960s! At around that time the US civil rights movement was gaining momentum and making strides to end segregation in the South. Martin Luther King Jr, had become a hero in Jamaica. It was hard to understand what was happening in the segregated US, where there were separate bathrooms and drinking fountains for blacks and whites in the South, while at my boarding school, black, brown, and a few white boys were sleeping in the same dorm, all sharing the same bathroom facilities. There we were, a cosmopolitan group of hungry schoolboys hunkered down at the long dining table, blithely unaware that beyond our shores there were places were a black man couldn't share a lunch counter with a white man.

I didn't feel I was any different than others in my home village of Epworth, St Ann. When I was at home on holiday from boarding school I'd spend time 'reasoning' (philosophizing) and playing dominoes with the labourers and peasant farmers while sucking on a couple Red Stripe beers. I was a few years underage, but that didn't matter in the only rum bar in the village. I remember my brother Andrew telling anyone who would listen, "Danny is trying to win a popularity contest."

In his own droll way, my brother had said something profound. I did want to be popular. Not popular in the normal way teenagers seek to impress their peers but to satisfy a need that was a curious bi-product of the society within which I lived. I was happy going to the polo club and mixing with my parents' friends or dancing at middle-class teenage parties, but for some reason, perhaps having to do with guilt, I also wanted to be part of another Jamaica. At times, my comfortable privilege felt like a guilty burden; I wanted to enter the other Jamaica where I felt at home among them in the rum bars, in the markets, and in the streets. There was something in their music and rhythm, their earthy wisdom and humour that made me feel forever rooted in Jamaica. They are totally fatalistic. A Rastaman in Negril once told me, "If you bawn fi heng, yu cyaan drown." If you were born to be hanged, you cannot drown. And I discovered that that too was my identity. So it wasn't just guilt. In spite of my whiteness, that's where I felt equally at home.

Back at the 'big house' one evening when I was sixteen or seventeen, I was sitting on the back verandah talking with my parents about racism, social justice, and the reforms that needed to take place now that Jamaica was an independent nation. Why was it, I railed, that a black Jamaican couldn't be a member of the Yacht Club or other social establishments, or could only get as far as accountant in our nation's banks? This was a colonial carry-over; no matter how qualified the black Jamaican employee was he or she could never become the branch manager, even in country towns like St Ann's Bay; that job was reserved for a Brit if the bank was Barclays, and a Canadian if it was the Bank of Nova Scotia.

I was on a roll. My mother, Janet, loved her G&Ts and more often than not she would have one too many on an evening. She listened intently to my equal rights and justice spiel that evening, eventually interrupting me to say: "I'm going to live to see the day when you have your father and I lined up against a wall and shot!" The conversation ended abruptly.

Maybe this is the exact moment in which my mother dropped a marker in her mind about who her youngest son was, as a person. Some of the most interesting insights that Toni shared with me were my mother's opinions on her sons. Bear in mind that these were shared with Toni when Janet was very old, but they were impressions that had crystallized over her lifetime.

To Toni, she hardly mentioned Bryan, who at age thirty-seven, committed suicide.

"With Chris," said Toni, "my take was that he was the child 'with the right hair and colour.' She was proud of him, proud that he played polo well, and proud that he went to Cornell, you know." Toni described the sadness Janet felt after he had his polo accident. "I might be being disrespectful to Ma, but I sensed that she wrote Chris off when she was told he would never be the same. Chris was, in her fantasy, going to be a shining success that she could bask in, but that was never going to be, so she just chucked him out of her sphere like a broken unwanted vase. She was always rough with him."

"Andrew was considered the good son," Toni continued. "She decided that when Pops died, Andrew was going to be her new Pops...only this time *she* would be holding the little suitcase with the money, and Andrew will be following orders. What a bunch of cartoon characters!"

Toni ended with me: "You were just a thief – you were a drug lord, AND you were going to send a HIT MAN to kill Andrew." Having never stolen, sold drugs (though I used), nor murdered anyone, I think these wild concerns expressed by my mother reflected a worry that began at that moment on the verandah witnessing the youthful exuberance of her rebel son. Interestingly, I was the son she called on for help in her later years.

I might have had an idea of what was going on in the world politically, but in terms of my studies, when I look back now I believe the dyslexia frustrated my success at school. I was a terrible student; the only subject I passed in high school final exams was West Indian History, and the only reason I passed was because I studied Rachel's notebooks the week before the exam. I rebelled to the point that the headmaster wrote my father and threatened to expel me. The teachers didn't know the half of it; not only were we going out to those dance halls at night, I and my group of like-minded rebels regularly smoked cigarettes and weed.

I left Jamaica College in the summer of 1965. My father arranged a job at Worthy Park Estate, a large sugar and cattle plantation in St Catherine. I was a junior overseer in the cattle division for the princely sum of eight pounds a week and lived in a small farmhouse. I spent several hours every weekday riding and tending the herds along with the cattlemen. My duties required me to visit the government agricultural station at Bodles in Old Harbour also in St Catherine where I learned to artificially inseminate and pregnancy test cattle; I became the sire of quite a few calves! After long days in the saddle we would stop at a village rum shop, tether the horses like cowboys at a western saloon, and drink rum and play dominoes until it got dark.

In 1966, Bostitch (my great-grandfather's American company) was sold to Textron. One year later, with a lot of encouragement from my older brother Bryan, who since university had been back in Jamaica for a number of years, Dad bought the first of a few companies mostly to do with auto service on the island – Tropical Battery Company and Jamaica Metal Refining, followed soon after by Birbari Limited, Caribrake and Tropical Service Stations Ltd.

It was at this time that I fell in love with my late first wife, Winsome. On the weekends if I didn't go to visit friends in Kingston, I would drive the winding narrow dirt road, more like a track really, through the mountains which was the shortest route to Ochi, the colloquial name for the north-coast tourist town of Ocho Rios. Byron Lee and the Dragonaires, a legendary band that helped popularize ska in the early days of Jamaican popular music, used to play poolside on a Sunday afternoon at the glamorous Hilton Hotel. Locals and tourists would gather to drink, dance, and enjoy the music. That's where I first laid eyes on Winsome Bowen. She was beautiful with a light brown complexion and a bright mocking smile that instantly challenged me. I admit I am a man who falls hard. We danced and that was it: I was in love. We soon became serious about each other, and I found myself in Ochi every weekend, sometimes driving back to Worthy Park at 3:00 a.m. on Monday morning and grabbing two hours sleep before going to work.

My parents and hers thought the romance was moving too fast, and I believe mine were apprehensive because Winsome was light brown. Suddenly, Winsome was sent off to England for a year while I was sent to a junior college in Oklahoma to study ranch management. That one year of college would be the extent of my tertiary education.

Arriving from Jamaica, I was not sure what to expect in rural Oklahoma in 1967. Eastern Oklahoma State College of about 1,500 students was situated on the edge of the little town of Wilburton, population about 2,000. It offered practical and vocational training, and I was there to study Ranch Operation, a one-year practical accredited course. It consisted of several field trips to working ranches or feed-lots and research stations. We learned how to run what the Okies called a 'cow calf operation', how to balance feed rations to get maximum weight gain, and other ranching best practices.

Looking back, you'd think I'd be aware of the significance of my going to my grandmother Berenice's country, reclaiming an American legacy about which I was perhaps curious or proud. But of course this was not so at all. I was just obliging my parents. I didn't have much ambition, probably because at the base of my psyche was that innate sense of financial well-being, the sense that like my father I'd always be able to coast on this magic but invisible carpet of safety the family money provided. I was there to get an education that might come in handy, but I didn't *need* to get an education. I didn't *need* a profession. And I was looking forward to getting college over with and getting back to my life in Jamaica and Winsome.

My most pleasant surprise was to find out that my small junior college had its own rodeo arena. Nothing fancy, mind you; it was more like a corral with stock chutes and a tiny bleacher stand. I would discover that many high schools in the state also had rodeo grounds. Rodeo was a mainstream sport like basketball or baseball in these parts. I had grown up with horses so I naturally enjoyed attending the rodeos, though where I came from we rode English style while everything there was American Western.

The popular pastime for all the students in my Ranch Operation course was chewing and dipping tobacco, or 'snuff'; it was part of the cowboy culture. Some of my colleagues would have a double dip, which was a pinch of moist, flavoured dipping tobacco placed between the gum and the lip with a wad of chewing tobacco in your cheek. Trying hard to be one of the boys I gave it my best shot, but I found it revolting, and if you inadvertently swallowed too much 'tobacco juice' you could be sick for days. The constant spitting was disgusting and when indoors the guys would use a Dixie cup to spit in. It was gross, but it was after all their culture. I skipped the chewing and stuck with the *Marlborough Man.*

My previous experience of America had been eastern cities, but I didn't really dwell on the contrast between those cities and the world I found here in Oklahoma. My touchstone of comparison would always be Jamaica and unfortunately the most vivid of these comparisons would be on the subject of race.

But my most profound enlightenment about Oklahoma wasn't going to be tobacco chewing or rodeos or even ranch operation. I wasn't altogether naïve; this was Oklahoma in the 1960s, and I knew there would be racism there though not necessarily against me as coming from Jamaica, I was a bit of a novelty being white. "How can you be a Jamaican and you're not black?" I got that question a lot back then, and sometimes still to this day.

I missed Winsome. The flame burned bright, and we wrote to each other daily that year, but I did make friends while in Oklahoma. Most of the college students were from neighbouring counties who drove home on the weekends, so the international students hung out on weekends. There were a few from Iran who all hated the Shah with a passion and two from Africa, one from Ghana, and the other from Nigeria, whom I befriended. I turned twenty within a month of arriving in Wilburton in 1967 and had worked for two years in Jamaica after leaving high school before going to college. I was accustomed to having a drink, and in this state the legal drinking age was twenty-one. There were only a couple of beer joints in town, so when I was 'carded' I'd immediately present my Jamaican driver's license, which back then was a little booklet and the bartenders would look at me then look at the photo and leaf through the booklet; it didn't occur to them there was no date of birth anywhere in it. I was good to go! This meant I could also buy beer for my friends who like me were all also underage. We would pick up a couple of six-packs and drive out to Robbers Cave State Park and brown bag it. The park had a series of caves that bandits of a bygone era used as their hideout, and a lake for swimming. It was popular on weekends, and pretty much the only attraction in the area.

One of the little beer joints I frequented was conveniently next door to the college. It was a square wooden structure much like a rum bar in rural Jamaica, with a couple of pool tables, a juke box, and a bar counter with a few stools. One Saturday night I was having a few beers there and a black guy stopped by to purchase a six-pack to go. I didn't really know the guy, but I'd seen him around as he worked as a groundsman at the college. He and a couple friends were on their way to McAlester, a much larger town about thirty miles away where they had a club for black people. I was familiar with the club they were going to visit as I'd been there with my African friends from the college. I had been the only white guy in the entire place. I remember seeing a few raised eyebrows and getting a couple *what the fuck are you doing in here white boy* looks, but no one said a word; they were cordial and we had a great evening listening and dancing to some sweet soul music from Otis Redding, Aretha Franklin, and Wilson Pickett.

Now at this beer joint closer to the college the bartender refused to serve the guy. I could not believe it. I intervened pleading with the bartender to sell him the beer and let him go on his way. The bartender began shouting at the man to get out or he would be thrown out. Maybe it was the beer, as I'm not really a fighter, but I told the bartender he would have to throw me out as well. In a flash one of the regulars who I knew casually, a pipeline welder by trade who everyone knew only as M.G., hit me with his pool cue and the next thing I knew I was flat on my face in the gravel car park. I crawled back to the campus licking my wounds.

I'd just had my first encounter with American racism up close and personal! The black population of Wilburton was only about one per cent, so I hadn't given a second thought as to why I'd never seen a black person in the place before; being from Jamaica it also never occurred to me that blacks were *not allowed* in the seedy little beer joint, the Civil Rights Act of 1964 notwithstanding.

Not all the students were cowboys, and not all were racists, either; my roommate George was from Anadarko, Oklahoma, billed as the Indian Capital of the Nation as there were more Native Americans than white people in the city. I spent a couple of weekends with him and his family there and have several fond memories of my year in Oklahoma. I also spent a weekend in Antlers with one of my classmates, an amateur bronc and bull rider. He had a wonderful, loving family and his mom cooked the best 'chicken-fried steak' I ever ate. His name was also Danny. He chewed tobacco all day and could hit a spittoon from ten feet away!

One of the sounds you are bound to hear if you spend any time in Oklahoma is the roar of a tornado. Coming from the Caribbean I was accustomed to hurricanes, so wasn't a tornado just a baby hurricane? No! It certainly wasn't. You can track a hurricane for days and either board up your house or get out of Dodge. Hurricanes are huge, a couple hundred miles across. A tornado is thin like a needle, it appears out of nowhere, and if you're lucky you get a few minutes' notice to take cover. I'd heard several harrowing tornado tales from my Oklahoma buddies and put most of them down to rum talk. Then one day I heard a rumbling so loud I about shit my pants; it was like ten freight trains bearing down – the loudest thunder you ever heard in a lightning storm, not in a burst of seconds but continuing for minutes that felt like eternity. The wind speed must have been 200 miles per hour. Suddenly, everybody in the dorm was shouting, and I was following the crowd down the stairway to the basement. Before I realized what had happened, it was all over. We went out to see the damage. The college had been spared, but the twister had surgically cut a narrow path about one hundred feet wide through a woodland just west of our dorm. Trees within the swathe of its reach were reduced to toothpicks, while trees outside of its path were untouched. I found this amazing.

The Vietnam War had a huge impact on the lives of American students back then. The vast majority saw it as a nonsensical war that could never be won, yet it had no end. Talk of the war depressed them; they spoke about it often, tempers flared, they cursed President Johnson and their government. As I've pointed out, the legal drinking age in Oklahoma was twenty-one, but the age for the draft was eighteen, and any student with less than a 3.0 GPA was conscripted into the army and shipped out to 'Nam. At eighteen years of age a student was old enough to die for his or her country but not old enough to hoist a beer to it! This really pissed off the students, and the subject would come up every time we went for a beer. George was one such student; his grades were not great so rather than be drafted he enlisted in the Navy with the hope of having a better chance of survival in that branch of the military.

Two years after I left Oklahoma, on one of the darkest days in American collegiate history, soldiers opened fire on a group of students at Kent State University in Ohio who were peacefully protesting the war; four were killed, and several were injured, some of the students shot were innocent bystanders. Within a few days four million outraged students from across the country held a student strike, which caught the attention of Congress, who began to cut the funding. It was a turning point, the beginning of the end of the war.

In the spring of 2008, forty years to the month after I had left Oklahoma, while on a road trip across America, Carole and I visited Wilburton; we drove through the little town and out to the college. The students had already left for the summer. We stopped at the administrative building and my old dorm and not much had changed in forty years. I have heard my friends speak about college reunions and the impact of this time in their life. Standing there in this place that now seemed so incidental to my life, I wondered how much more I would have valued it if I hadn't carried with me to college my own security blanket: the knowledge of the Briggs fortune made in a far off eastern state of this country.

I completed my college year in Oklahoma and returned to Jamaica. If our parents thought the separation might have cooled down the love affair between me and Winsome, it didn't; if ever the adage 'absence makes the heart grow fonder' was true, this was our experience. Add that to our Romeo and Juliet syndrome and it only made us more determined. We resumed the relationship the moment we returned to Jamaica.

I was not too concerned about life; my dad's money was supposedly endless. I returned from college and worked for a while on the family farm at Arthur's Seat, a farm that never turned a profit. Winsome and I got married in April 1969. Dad helped us with a house on the property, where we would raise our three sons, Marc, Alexander, and Daniel junior. Winsome, or 'Chummie' as she was known to friends, had an unconditional love for her three boys. They could do no wrong in her eyes. Over the years my parents especially my mother grew to love Chummie.

The early 1970s was a period of massive and fundamental change for Jamaica and its people. Michael Manley, my friend Rachel's father, won a handsome victory at the polls in 1972 to become prime minister having campaigned on a platform of social reform. It was needed! There was an undercurrent from the disenfranchised and a budding Black Power movement that gave one the feeling that Jamaica was a powder keg waiting to explode.

Then came the oil crisis in 1973, the formation of OPEC and the quadrupling of gas prices that triggered a world recession. Jamaica had zero oil, but it did have huge reserves of bauxite, the ore used to make aluminium. Manley saw an opportunity to renegotiate the levy paid by the overseas mining companies, to which those companies cried foul. Whereas the US could do nothing about OPEC, they could easily punish Jamaica. And they did. It didn't help that Manley had defied the US by developing a relationship with our closest Caribbean neighbour, Cuba, and when he paid Fidel Castro an official visit, America labelled Manley a communist. Manley's response to all the hysteria on his return from Cuba was an intemperate public remark he'd live to regret: "If you don't like it, there are five flights a day to Miami." Many upper-class Jamaicans took him literally and fled the country.

Jamaica was split down the middle; half the people loved Manley, and the other half hated him. Pearnel Charles, a political rival, once said of Michael that if you wanted to continue to hate the man don't talk to him, because if you did, you'd change your mind. I knew Michael quite well through Rachel. I liked the man; he was cool, he used to take us all out in the Olds Super 88, and later the Buick Electra 225 – how do I even remember the models of his cars to this day? I would say we were all in awe of him back then. I remember the huge scandal when a reporter for the *Gleaner*'s afternoon rag, *The Star*, caught Michael at a house with another man's wife. I thought this all very risqué and daring; these kinds of things make a strong impression on a teenager. I would *not* like him as much in the late 1970s when he allowed the far left to take over the party.

In light of the serious economic blows sustained by the island, the propaganda war was unbelievable, the economy tanked, and many people panicked; wealthy Jamaicans went to extraordinary lengths to move their money to Miami and tax havens like the

Cayman Islands. Next, they sold their homes, packed, and fled the country.

Mine was one such family. When my parents and siblings fled the island, I took over the Jamaican businesses my father had invested in earlier, and took advantage of the exodus by buying a few of the fire-sale properties that had become abundant on the market.

Maybe it was my exposure to the rank and file of Jamaica, to their culture and ganja and music, their poverty and politics, but I could never imagine myself anywhere else. My roots were unconscious and deep. I had a privileged background, but every inch of my psyche and personality was Jamaican. My family might have wandered through various diasporas that led to Jamaica, but all I knew was this small island, 146 miles long and 51 miles wide, with its brooding Blue Mountains, winding country roads, calamitous cities thundering with reggae music, and its relentless waterfalls, cream-coloured beaches, and embracing Caribbean waters.

As the '70s came to a close, political tribalism reared its ugly head, violence raged, and gangs affiliated to both political parties fought for turf in the streets of Kingston. The emergence of a radical left-wing fringe in Manley's party didn't help matters as the economy collapsed. But I still wasn't going anywhere. I reasoned that Jamaica couldn't become communist for two reasons: one, Michael Manley for all his sins was committed to the Westminster model of democracy, and two, I was convinced Jamaicans were too colourful, independent, and undisciplined to be communists. In my lifetime, I'd never even seen a Jamaican so much as form a tidy queue for a bus.

In 1980 the gun violence peaked, and some 800 Jamaicans lost their lives; it was a scary time. The propaganda and rumour-mongering became relentless in light of a crumbling economy.

Supermarket shelves stood empty. Shortages and strict curtailment on taking or sending money abroad led to predictions that Jamaica would end up like Cuba. The presence of well-meaning Cubans in the island sent by a friendly government to assist with building schools and modernizing agriculture, and with sending doctors for rural hospitals, didn't help the rising hysteria. Fearing for the safety of my wife and children, I moved them to Florida, and visited them for about a week each month.

It was obvious that the US administration, aided and abetted by the Opposition Jamaica Labour Party (JLP) were destabilizing the elected government of Jamaica and in the process driving Manley out of office. The propaganda was unrelenting, Jamaicans were led to believe that under Manley, Jamaica was bound to become a communist state. The campaign worked.

In Jamaica we always felt that a fear of communism was what motivated the US hysteria over the Manley socialist government. But a mountain of 'empirical evidence' from declassified documents from several agencies, including the CIA, FBI, and the NSC reveals a different motive. Their assessment of the spread of communism in the Caribbean and Jamaica in particular, resulted in the State Department soliciting a political profile of Prime Minister Manley from British intelligence that referred to Manley as "a leader who is neither a Marxist nor a revolutionary". So the allegation that Manley was a communist and that Jamaica embraced communism, was undiluted US propaganda, manufactured for Jamaican consumption.

Declassified documents of the former Soviet Union show they had no interest in cultivating ideological or political-military ties with Manley. They already had Cuba in the region which was costing them a fortune.

So what was the source of their hatred for Manley's Government? State Department papers reveal their concern about how democratic socialism in Jamaica highlighted class distinctions and empowered black people there, which could spread to the rest of the Caribbean. Because of its size, population, and aggressive confidence, Jamaica under any type of regime would be a power factor in the English-speaking Caribbean. It exercises a role and influence there and in the Third World disproportionate to its small size.

Jamaica has always punched above its weight – our athletes, Marcus Garvey and our music which became the sound-track of social protest around the world. Our influence was feared from the time of slavery by colonizers and Christian missionaries. As they say, *Jamaica is a very big country on a small island.*

Manley lost the election at the end of 1980, and a few years later, my wife and children returned home. I had actually benefited from the chaos, as property values skyrocketed after the government changed. But as a family we paid a price for our separation. The period of estrangement had caused us damage, and Winsome and I eventually divorced. As it is with these things, sadly, it's the kids to whom the cost is greatest.

5

The Quest for Great-Grandfather Briggs

I was always aware that I was from a wealthy family, but how that came about remained vague in my mind as a child growing up in colonial Jamaica. The source of my family's wealth was to me nothing more than a sketchy collection of odd and mostly unconnected details I'd gleaned over the years and an occasional visit from some distant relative from America or from farther away. All that seemed to matter was that the name Briggs provided me with that unspoken certainty that whatever the history of that name was, and its connection to the Melville name, it had made us privileged and safe financially. But after that Arlington visit in 2018, I started to look into that history. Yes, it's true that it took until I was in my seventies to start digging, but better late than never – and I was richly rewarded for it. In fact, reaching out to my extended family was a big help, too; as soon as I informed them of my project, a floodgate of memories and memorabilia opened as though they had all been waiting for someone to start the process.

It's amazing how, when one starts searching around and asking questions, all sorts of unexpected gems of information turn up.

A newspaper edition on June 20, 1957, *The Rhode Island Pendulum* (later the *East Greenwich Pendulum*) declared that week 'Bostitch Week' to celebrate the return of Bostitch to East Greenwich. One of many articles describes Thomas Briggs its founder as typifying the traditional American success story, calling him an 'inventive genius'.

And in a recording from a 1971 radio programme from WJAR Radio in Providence, Rhode Island, sent to me by my cousin Marianne in Cape Cod, I quote from it in part:

> *His original ideas created a giant industry. These are extracts from the story of* A Rhode Island Portrait in Sound.
>
> *He began an industry that's known today as Bostitch...*
>
> *His first creation was a label machine...a most successful invention...still used today with relatively little change. But always in the back of his mind was the desire to design a wire stitching machine that could be used for book binding....(He) developed a machine that could be instantly adjusted by a slight turn of a crank. He called his machine The Boston Wire Stitcher...*
>
> *During WWI his talents were called on by the government....He produced a machine to manufacture a gun cartridge belt and another to load the belt with 300 shells, the entire operation taking exactly 1 minute.*
>
> *But of course the brightest spot in the company's history was the introduction of the simple stapler that millions of people use every day.*
>
> *A Rhode Island Portrait in Sound.*
Written and narrated by Florence Markoff.

Forty-three years after Thomas Briggs's death, they were still talking about him in Rhode Island. Let's start at the beginning. Thomas Briggs was born January 19, 1857, in Little Compton, Rhode Island, the son of Samuel Albert Briggs and his wife Lucy Ann Rice. Lucy was of aristocratic stock from Warwick, the state's second-largest city; her mother was a member of the genteel

Northrop family. Samuel was in the booming Providence jewellery business, and he had his own shop until 1861 when the market was destroyed in the mid-nineteenth century by the Civil War. Samuel's business folded along with many other jewellery shops forcing him to move into full-time farming in the village of Little Compton.

I am not a believer in astrology, but early in my search I was struck by the discovery that Thomas Briggs was born under the sign of Capricorn. This is a sign known for its practical approach; the application of intelligence and logic to solve problems. And in a sense that was exactly what Thomas Briggs was: a problem solver. His inventions all served to make everyday challenges and even extraordinary ones easier.

Initially, I could not find much about his childhood in Little Compton other than the fact that Thomas grew up on a farm and attended public school there. Little Compton still has only one school today, The Wilbur & McMahon School, which would then have been the Josephine F. Wilbur School, a much smaller version. I discovered that by 1747 Little Compton, once part of the Plymouth colony and boasting residents from as far back as the *Mayflower*, had been absorbed by Rhode Island. In 1857 Little Compton had a population of around 1,400 people, 98 per cent of whom were white. It was known for the Sakonnet Light Station on its rocky coast and home of Rupert von Trapp, son of the famous Trapp Family Singers who inspired the movie *The Sound of Music*. And Little Compton was the only place in America with a granite monument to a chicken – it is home to the famous Rhode Island Red breed.

At sixteen, young Thomas was employed by the local pharmacist in the small village of Centreville, where he remained for three years selling dry goods owing to the fact that he was not a licensed pharmacist. Having gained sufficient experience in the field of pharmaceuticals, Thomas opened his own pharmaceutical business in nearby Pepperell, Massachusetts. When I think about it, I can't help wondering how at nineteen this young man was able to envision his own business in this very specialized field and raise the financing to start it so quickly. It showed guts and an early flair for business.

He operated his pharmaceutical business for two years, but as he became increasingly impatient with the tedious and time-consuming process of labelling containers, Thomas created a device that would do this labelling swiftly and automatically. Then, having perfected his labelling machine, Thomas patented it in 1882 when he was only twenty-five years old, establishing the Rhode Island Label Works in Providence on Sabin Street.

This was evidently a watershed experience for Thomas in more ways than one. He promptly sold his business in Pepperell and decided to devote his time from then on to a career of invention and manufacturing. On April 4, 1878, at the age of twenty-one, Thomas married Alice Fuller in Pepperell. She was only seventeen at the time and within a year she bore them a daughter, Helen. Another eleven years would pass before a second child, my grandmother Berenice, was born in 1890 by which time Thomas had moved his family to Medford Street in Arlington.

Let me set the scene of the place in history when Berenice was born. It was the beginning of what was known as The Progressive Era of America lasting from 1890 to 1920. The so-called Gilded Age of industrialization in the US had raised standards of living for many, while corporate bosses, referred to as 'robber barons', pursued unethical and unfair business practices aimed at eliminating competition and increasing profits. Factory workers, many of them recent immigrants, were frequently subjected to brutal and perilous working and living conditions. Political corruption enriched politicians, and the gap between the 'haves' and the 'have-nots' was widening.

Thomas Briggs was developing his business during this exciting period in American history, so I felt compelled to understand it a bit better. Progressive Era reformers sought to regulate private industry, strengthen protections for workers and consumers, expose corruption in both government and big business, and generally improve society. Though many noteworthy goals were achieved, within the movement there was a very dark side, as some reformers promoted discriminatory policies and espoused intolerant ideas. The Woodrow Wilson administration (1913 –21), despite its embrace of modernity and progress, pursued a racial agenda that culminated in the segregation of the federal government. It witnessed a revival of the Ku Klux Klan and a viciously racist backlash against the economic and political gains of African Americans in the post-Reconstruction period.

Worse, it was so-called Progressive 'reformers' who embraced 'the science of better breeding'. The Eugenics Movement espoused a totally racist and classist hierarchy that placed white, Anglo-Saxon Protestants at the top, and lower classes, ethnic minorities, recent immigrants, and the mentally ill at the bottom. In 1907, the US became the first country to pass a compulsory sterilization law. The genocidal policies of Nazi Germany ultimately discredited the 'science' of eugenics, but not before more than 60,000 American men and women were forcibly sterilized to prevent them from having children. I can't help wondering if it was the Progressive Era or Medieval Era? Seems it was a mixture of both.

But let's return to my great-grandfather's story. Imagine inventing a product at age nineteen that would provide enough money to allow complete independence at such a young age! The label machine, the original source of his success as an inventor, and whose patent he later sold remained in use up to 1971 with very few changes. This young man's ability to bring practical logic to bear on problem-solving would prove to be Thomas's rare gift, and the list of his inventions he'd go on to mastermind is a substantial one.

The Boston Globe featured Briggs's latest invention, the paper feeder. (It was highly praised again almost a century later in the 1984 issue of *The American Stationer.*) Thomas was making a modest name for himself in Boston and beyond.

A major breakthrough for Thomas in being recognized for his invention skills came when he was commissioned by the Carter-Crume Company, now the American Sales Book Company, to invent and build several special-type high-speed machines for printing and binding. These were the first machines to combine the many processes necessary in the manufacture of the books they were selling, and he installed them for Carter-Crume on a special agreement. These innovations proved to be a resounding success, assuring him a comfortable income that allowed him to dedicate his life and talents from here on to invention and manufacturing.

The perfecting of the wire-stitching machines that were marketed through the American Type Founders' Company was the springboard for the establishment of the Boston Wire Stitcher Company in 1896, with Thomas as its president. In the early years Thomas had been working his industrial magic in the garage I'd later see at Medford Street in Arlington, Massachusetts, but in 1900 the company bought a plant in East Greenwich, Rhode Island, and began the mass manufacture of these machines. By 1904 he had outgrown that first move and bought a huge old mill that is still standing today. This latest move was a risky one; the plant was obviously much bigger than he needed at the time, and he moved there having eighty employees and created such a debt burden that at one point he couldn't make his payroll.

Thomas's answer was to invent himself out of this dilemma. In addition to the wire-stitcher, which would lead to his inventing the modern stapler, the company launched into the machine for securing window shades to rollers, a paper-feeder for larger presses (1892) whose patent he sold probably because the wire-stitcher was so expensive to manufacture that it prevented him also entering the paper feeder field, and various machines and appliances for use in printing, all invented by him. His genius for the mechanical flourished, and his company prospered under his equally gifted business leadership. In the years leading up to the First World War, Thomas was in his mid-50s and overseeing his company's offices, which had spread beyond the US as far as Canada, Cuba, and South America.

Thomas may have been too old to serve at the front, but in the War from 1914 to 1918 his expertise would serve the allied forces cause in other invaluable ways. He was pressed into service by the Ordnance Department to redesign the original gun cartridge belt whose delivery was not only inefficient but also costly to manufacture. After a careful study of the problems, Thomas and his associates came up with two machines to manufacture his new design: one for a superior belt and another to load it with 300 shells, allowing the entire operation of reloading to be completed in one minute. Produced in Thomas Briggs's factory, this machinery was shipped to ammunition plants throughout the country for use in the manufacture of machine-gun belts and shells, in a more efficient and more cost-effective process – and more lethal. It is interesting to note that during the Second World War Bostitch was once again pressed into service to assist in the war effort and produced twenty million square yards of camouflage netting and manufactured 200,000 Browning automatic rifles in its facilities.

The company remained in this location for thirty-two years, justifying Thomas's initial faith. It wasn't until eighteen years after Thomas's death on September 24, 1928, that Bostitch finally outgrew that building and moved to Connecticut. But in 1957 it would return to East Greenwich with a new plant, the one I would visit in 1958 with my family when I was a kid.

So, yes, the invention of the wire stitcher was the one that got Thomas Briggs started and cemented his success; it was the reason he called the company he founded in 1896 the Boston Wire Stitcher Company. Then came Thomas Brigg's foot-operated wire stitcher invention in 1903, a new way to bind books, which led three years later to his Bostitch Model A staple binder that used the first preformed staples on tin cores. He produced the Bostitch Model AO stapler in 1914, a compact design with simplified loading allowing more widespread use. And then in 1923 the Bostitch Model B-1 Desk Stapler came into the business world. It was an affordable, stamped steel construction and was the first to use a coiled spring.

But to me, the invention that I have always associated with my great-grandfather was not the wire stitcher, but the good old stapler. I can remember as a child seeing Bostitch staplers everywhere in Jamaica and feeling great pride in that simple machine that replaced the paper clips and rubber bands, the gluing or wax stamps that cluttered people's desks. There was not only a stapler in every office and most homes, there were commercial and industrial products in every hardware store including roofing staplers and even nailing guns.

I clearly remember a young lawyer friend of my older brother who worked in an old and very prestigious Kingston law firm. He knew of our family's association with Bostitch and complained to my dad that while the device worked very well, it was large and heavy compared to the smaller staplers available on the market; the law firm was still using a Bostitch model designed and manufactured in the 1930s, and this was the mid-1960s, a testament to its quality. This made me feel so proud.

So who was Thomas Briggs outside of his work? As far as his social life, I couldn't find a lot in the papers. There are many mentions in the local Boston press of Alice attending weddings and other social engagements, though Thomas and the children are not mentioned much. I guess Thomas was a workaholic and in those days kids were usually in the home.

In 1903 there is mention in *The Rhode Island Pendulum* of social engagements attended by Thomas and his daughter Berenice, and Thomas's purchase of 'Phoenix Mill', the property that would eventually house the headquarters for the Boston Wire Stitcher Company. *The Worcester Skandinavia*, a paper printed in Swedish for the Swedish immigrants in New England, announced Thomas's purchase of the 'Phoenix Woolen Mill of East Greenwich', with an offer of $500 annual salary to any immigrant Swedes who wished to relocate and work for the Boston Wire Stitcher Company. In early 1904, Thomas Briggs moved his family from Arlington and in March of that year there is mention of Thomas leasing the home of a deceased member of the wealthy Spencer family to use for his family when they were in Rhode Island. (An interesting footnote: the Spencer family were ancestors of Diana Spencer, who'd be Princess of Wales.)

What I do know from various family members was that Thomas loved fast cars, particularly Oldsmobiles. It is said he bought a new

Girl stapling beats girl taping 15 to 1

This is a race between two girls in an air filter manufacturing plant.

Both girls are skilled at assembling the frames and outer screens which hold the filtrant. One girl uses tape. The other uses an electrically powered Bostitch stapler.

In the time it takes the girl taping to complete *one* filter, the girl stapling finishes 15. The result — extra profit — and a better product.

Winnings come in other ways, too. Stapled filters are neater looking and more uniform. Every staple grips securely for strength where it's needed. There's less operator fatigue, and no special operator training or skill is required.

The stapler in this race is one of more than 800 made by Bostitch to cut fastening costs in production lines, shipping rooms and offices. The staple is one of more than 200 Bostitch types.

Finding the right combination of stapler and staple to cut your costs and increase your profits is a job for the Bostitch Economy Man. Over 350 of these fastening experts are in 123 U. S. and Canadian cities.

Call in your nearest one to study your fastening methods. No obligation. He'll tell you honestly if stapling can save you money.

Look up "Bostitch" in your phone book or write us.

FREE Bulletins that tell you how stapling saves time and money for others

Fasten it better and faster with

Bostitch, 461 Briggs Drive, East Greenwich, Rhode Island

I want to fasten

☐ wood   ☐ plastics   ☐ cartons   ☐ leather
☐ rubber ☐ light metals ☐ fabric   ☐ roofing

Name_____

Company_____

City_____Zone_____State_____

model every year or two. The curved-dash Olds, one-cylinder, became a commercial sensation after appearing in the 1901 New York Auto Show. It was one of the first true mass-produced automobiles and would have caught Thomas's eye given his love of innovation and making useful tools or in this case modern transport available to everyone. In 1905, the company rolled out its first two-cylinder car, leading up to the four-cylinder car in later models.

Maybe each new, speedy Oldsmobile drove Thomas further away from what would later be discovered to be an unhappy home life and was the final proverbial straw that broke Alice's back, and the back of her husband's patience and dedication. But tragedy struck the family in 1906. Their older daughter, my great-aunt Helen, then married to Dana Lawrence with three small children, died tragically at just twenty-seven years of age. Berenice would have been only sixteen when she lost her big sister. Perhaps this brought Alice and Thomas closer for a while, though it may have contributed to their final split, which was to come some ten years later. The house on Medford Street, listed under Alice's name, was sold the year Helen died and the family moved to Rhode Island.

Thomas became community-minded on his return to his native Rhode Island. In 1910, along with other wealthy residents he attended a meeting of the Union Trust Company at its Providence, RI, office at which they agreed to work towards the 'civic betterment' of East Greenwich. Two months later the East Greenwich Board of Trade was created (later becoming the East Greenwich Chamber of Commerce in 1916). In 1912 Thomas was elected to the Trades and Manufacturing committee, becoming its chairman a year later. It was charged with locating sites for new local manufacturing plants.

Thomas also dabbled in local politics. After numerous discussions with town residents about how they could make a permanent mark, Thomas helped found a social club for the Warwick Republicans in 1914 led by an executive committee of which Thomas was a member. He was also elected to the Warwick Town Council in 1913, and re-elected in 1914, becoming its president, though he resigned before the expiration of his term. Did the social club Thomas helped found leave much of a mark? It's impossible to know, but is interesting to note that Republicans controlled party politics in Rhode Island for the next twenty years.

In addition to cars and motoring, Thomas loved golf, and he was fond of all outdoor sports. He maintained a residence at 60 South Angell Street in Providence, and may have had a winter home in St Augustine, Florida. He also bought a home in Altamonte Springs, Florida, another winter escape, which is mentioned in his 1917 will. Altamonte Springs was a tiny village back then and is now one of the northern suburbs of Orlando. Five guys from Boston had created a development there – a hotel and lots for sale. Thomas bought land and used to stay at the hotel.

It seemed that it was around this time that his marriage may have started to break down. I learned that Alice, who is said to have constantly lorded it over Thomas that she was a distant descendant of Ulysses Grant and the *Mayflower*, was often described as a miserable woman who smoked two cartons of cigarettes a week, and constantly nagged him over his 'hobbies'. The story goes that on one occasion when Thomas extended the garage to house a new Oldsmobile, Alice put him out the house and told him to go and live with his inventions and his new car.

Although the couple remained in close contact, Thomas established residence in Reno, Nevada, and on November 21, 1916, and in a suit brought by Thomas for 'cruel treatment', a divorce was granted with alimony for Alice. Thomas wasted no time in marrying a second time, to one Esther Knight, on February 7, 1917, in Rhode Island. It is fairly obvious that Thomas had been having an affair with Esther while married to Alice, as they got married less than three months after his divorce. In those days Reno required residency for one year before a divorce could be granted; with his creative mind, Thomas discovered a way around that stumbling block, for he never lived there for a year.

But who was Thomas Briggs really? I wanted a glimpse of my great-grandfather's heart. There is little to go on, but I found a touching note he wrote from Altamonte Springs in 1921 to his granddaughter, Helen's daughter Marian:

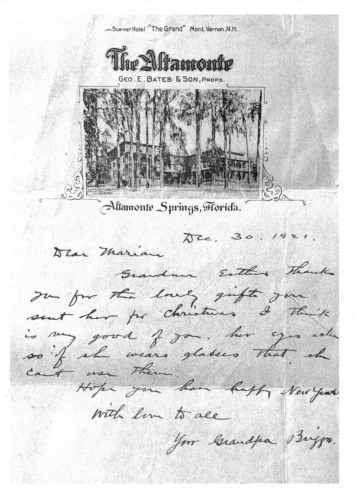

Grandma Esther is of course Thomas's second wife. Esther Knight was a twice-widowed Rhode Island socialite. She had no children with her first two husbands, and no doubt she was available and fancy free for Thomas and his outdoor activities. Esther was active in many Providence charitable organizations until her death in 1942, fourteen years after Thomas's. Coincidentally his first wife Alice Briggs also died that year.

Thomas may have found late-life happiness with Esther, but it's his marriage to Alice that's important for us, his descendants, today. Despite their divorce in 1916, he and Alice remained amicable, as she always stayed geographically close to Thomas – a few minutes away in East Greenwich. She never married again, and when she died in 1942, she was buried next to her daughter Helen. Her tombstone includes the words, 'Wife of Thomas Briggs'.

I deeply admire Thomas's entrepreneurship. I am not an inventor like him, not in the sense of machinery and equipment. If I have inherited a creative bent, it is possibly his flair for entrepreneurship, and an instinct to do things on my own and in my own way as well as an imaginative streak that allows me to think outside the box and, though not mechanically minded, to solve logistical problems.

Perhaps it's a bit strange, but there is something that struck me as I immersed myself more deeply in whatever history was available on Thomas Briggs. Growing up on his father's farm in Little Compton, a place known for rearing the famous Rhode Island Red Chickens, my great-grandfather's earliest memories of home may have featured the sight of a backyard, teeming with those busy, broody creatures. The ideas awakened my own earliest memory in rural Jamaica. I was too young to remember living in Kingston, but in January 1952 when I was four years old and my father moved the family to Arthur's Seat, I do recall the day we moved. It was rainy and cold by Jamaican standards, and I was worried about a bunch of young speckled chickens in a small wire mesh cage on top of the truck. They were soaked to the bone after the long drive from the city, and we put them in front of the old black iron Caledonia wood stove in the kitchen to dry out their coats of feathers.

6

Helen Briggs

*I*t is said no parent should live to see the death of their child. Thomas Briggs would live to see the death of one, and Alice would live to see the death of both. Helen Ethelwynn was born on January 28, 1879, eleven years before her sister Berenice, my grandmother.

Given their age difference, the sisters were unlikely to have had a close relationship. That's only an assumption, though, as we have little information on either of the girls during their growing up years. Whereas there are many mentions in *The Boston Globe* between the years 1880 and 1930 of Alice Briggs appearing at weddings and engagements, and Thomas has been mentioned often as a well-known businessman, there's almost nothing about the children. Other than Helen's wedding in February 1897, there is only one other notice of Helen, and that is about a piano recital. There is also a single mention in *The Rhode Island Pendulum* in 1908 when Berenice attended a church social held at the First Baptist Church in East Greenwich.

Why do I find it strange that there are so few mentions? Perhaps because as children of wealthy, successful, and well-connected parents I imagined they would be young debutantes welcomed at everyone's ball. But clearly the Briggs family lived a fairly low-key family life; perhaps Thomas and Alice brought their daughters up under that old conservative adage that children should only be seen, not heard.

At age 18, Helen got married to Dana Lawrence. The announcement in the *Arlington Advocate* on February 12, 1897 reads:

The eldest daughter of Mr. and Mrs. T.A. Briggs, Miss Helen Ethelwynn, was quietly married at home on Medford Street, Wednesday at 11 am, the happy bridegroom being Mr. Dana Lawrence, the youngest son of Mr. Henry L. Lawrence, one of Arlington's most respected citizens. The ceremony was performed by Rev. Frederick Gill of the Unitarian Church. The bride, a pretty, slender blonde, was attired in a myrtle green broadcloth travelling costume and carried a bouquet of lilies of the valley. She wore a broach of pearls and diamonds, the gift of the bridegroom, and she in turn presented him with a pear-shaped pearl scarf pin. The house was tastefully decorated with lilies and other flowers. Following the marriage a dainty lunch was served and then the couple departed on a brief wedding tour. They will be at home at 87 Medford St., to their friends after March 1st. The presents included a quantity of table silver, some handsome lamps, choice French clock, cut glass, oak dressing case and a rich case of silver, containing sets of spoons, forks and knives of the various sizes, the gift of Mr. and Mrs. T.W. Lawson, a lifelong friend of the wife's father. (The newspaper was wrong on one point: they were actually going to be 'at home to their friends' at number 57, not number 87, Medford Street. Dana lived just down the road from the Briggs.)

Dana Lawrence was the youngest son of a wealthy bank executive and had met Helen while working at Boston's Faneuil

Hall Marketplace. After their February 1897 wedding they remained in Arlington and by December 2 that same year their daughter, Marian, was born. The union later produced two sons, Robert in 1899 and Leonard in 1901. The new family of five moved to Belfast, Maine, in 1901, where Dana bought a dairy farm. They would remain there until 1906 when Thomas Briggs, missing his daughter and his new grandchildren, asked the family to return to East Greenwich, and that Dana work with him at Bostitch.

Dana did indeed return to Rhode Island to work for his father-in-law, initially leaving Helen and the children in Belfast. A handwritten document from a woman named Anna Mathewson – a key figure here, as she would be the children's schoolteacher and then Dana's second wife – gives us a picture of the time:

> *When Dana and Helen were breaking up their home in Belfast – Mr. Briggs, Helen's father came to them with the conditions in the new factory in East Greenwich. He had mortgaged the property for all that it would carry, The American Type Founders Co. had extended credit and yet he could not meet his payroll. …. I could picture the group in the little farm house. Helen says, "Don't do it for my sake!" when Dana arranged to let Mr. Briggs have $2,500 for which he gave a second mortgage on the real estate and the promise of 2 cents per case of staple if Dana would move to EG and take over the staple department. This was the turn of the tide for the B.W.S.Co. In August the goods were packed and Dana and Marian came to EG… Helen and the boys came in September having stayed in Belfast with friends until the freight car arrived with their household goods.*

Dana, himself from a wealthy family, had rescued an over-extended Thomas Briggs with a loan. But the new family chapter had hardly begun when tragedy struck. The local newspaper had an account, of sorts, of Helen's death at age twenty-seven. It stated that despite her *"being out calling on friends Wednesday evening,"*

Helen was suffering from "*nervous debility to some extent.*"(Whatever that means.) Then it goes on: *Early Thursday morning* [September 20, 1906] *she was taken ill, and Doctor Taggart was called. He did not consider her condition alarming, however, but during the afternoon heart failure ensued, and caused her death.* The cause of death was in fact recorded as an embolism, and, "*The funeral services were held at her late residence Saturday afternoon at 2 o'clock.*"

In 2019, I spoke with Marianne Hirschman, who is Helen's great-granddaughter, about Helen's death, and she had a rather different account. In fact, she imparted a dark family secret. "One day," Marianne shared with me, "Helen told Anna Mathewson, the children's teacher, that she had an appointment in Boston and would be gone for the day. When Helen returned she was deathly ill, and kept her eldest child, Marian, who was eight at the time, at home to help care for her." But within hours, Helen had died of peritonitis, an inflammation of the abdomen wall. Dr. Taggart, Alice, Berenice, and Helen's husband, Dana, were with her when she died. What Marianne said next shocked me: "You see, she had had an abortion in Boston. I never knew this until Grandma Marian died. It's a very sad, tragic story that affected many lives." She then handed me a photocopy of the now ancient letter written by the teacher Anna Mathewson. Written many years later, it's a fuller account that also paints a picture of the Lawrence family at the time.

> *Helen brought the children to the Cowesett School during the morning session of school on September 12th, a Wednesday. Marian, 8, Robert, 6, and Leonard, 5, were entered in the primary room – four grades, every desk and chair filled. Leonard remembers being given a pencil and a piece of paper and....punching holes into the paper was his first busy work while his mother and the teacher reminisced experiences as pupils*

at Friends School. Helen had attended from 1894-1896, and I from 1898 to 1902, so while we had never met, many of the teachers... were mutually ours. Discipline in that bee-hive was remarkably good that morning as I remember, the teacher's eyes quelling various corners of mischief. As Helen was about to leave, after stating that she was planning to be in a Boston hospital [soon] for a slight operation, she said, "I'm leaving the children with you – I know you will have an oversight over them and there'll be a housekeeper at the house." How prophetic her words were to become she did not dream!

Dana had begun the task of making staples on an unpatented machine. A new machine, an imperfect machine. Dana who knew next to nothing about machinery, whose only mechanical experience had been guns, a motorboat and briefly farm machinery. Dana who except for a few years had followed strict hours in his father's business in Quincy Market now began work at 7 a.m. till 6 p.m. with an hour at noon. His one relaxation, the motorboat, had arrived and was in the cove. In the hours after work and on Sundays Helen and the children were on the water with him.

I never talked to Helen after that morning she brought the children to school, but just a week later I saw her and the two blond little boys with scarlet caps on Main Street. They were going out in the boat for their last sail together.

The next morning Marian didn't come to school and Robert explained Mom was sick, so Marian stayed to help. I learned later that Helen had been taken ill early that morning, that Dr. Taggart procured Elizabeth Weld, a registered nurse. Whatever the conditions – symptoms or pain – no one doctor, nurse or family realized the seriousness; at one o'clock Helen was great apparently and Dana asked Miss Weld if it would be all right for him to go back to the shop, his mind on the work there. Miss Weld assured him she and Marian could care for everything.

A little later Helen complained of her limbs being cold and asked to put her feet in hot mustard water. Miss Weld took her pulse and then realized its weakened beat. Hastily she called Dana; Berenice and Mr. Briggs came, and at 4 o'clock life ebbed away. Embolism was the doctor's report.

First act was to send for Rev Wm Vaughn, pastor at the Dutch Reformed Church in Belfast, which Helen had helped to build. The Vaughns had been dear and intimate friends during the years both Lawrences & Vaughns lived near each other. Mr. Vaughn had been pastor of the Collegiate Church in NY City but his health failing he returned to Maine.

Had it been feasible Dana would have held the funeral the day following Helen's death.... But the following Saturday was decided upon, so Mr. Vaughn would be able to take the boat from Boston in time for his Sunday service.

But the funeral, which was a very private affair, was held at Helen's home on the following Saturday at 2:00 p.m. The service was conducted by their personal pastor, Revd Vaughn, who travelled down from Belfast, Maine. Dana, Thomas, Alice, and Berenice signed a letter that appeared under the obituary:

We wish to express our sincere thanks to our friends for their kindness and sympathy during our recent bereavement.

The next public mention of Helen would come fifty years later. The newspaper again carried a repeat of the death notice on October 4, 1956, as part of a "50 years ago" feature. To be remembered fifty years later for the anniversary of her death speaks to either Helen's lasting importance to the community or that of the family.

But back to Anna's letter – something she wrote stuck in my mind and still haunts me. When, just before Helen left the children at the school, she turned to Anna and said: *"I am leaving the children with you. I know you'll have an oversight over them and there'll be a housekeeper at the house."* And Anna's comment: *"How prophetic her words were to become she did not dream!"*

Bearing in mind that in those days abortion was not only illegal but considered immoral and firmly frowned upon by church and society, this comment may not only reflect the fact that the children had relocated and would be coming full-time to this school, but it may also give us a glimpse into Helen's state of mind as she faced what in those days would have been a 'back-street' operation at best. Perhaps she feared that something bad might happen and she'd no longer be there for her children. Or maybe Helen's comment was just a canny woman's instinct. For by the time Anna Mathewson wrote this letter, she was already Dana Lawrence's second wife.

The shadow of Helen's death in 1906 would have no doubt hovered darkly over the Briggs household especially Berenice who at sixteen would have felt a pall over her teenage years. Indeed, there is a possibility she didn't return to school after her sister's death. There is a mention in September 1906 of her being a student at East Greenwich Academy, a Methodist boarding high school in East Greenwich, despite her parents being Baptists, but there is no record of her graduating. At the time, American law mandated children had to be in school only up to age sixteen.

Then six years later, when Berenice was twenty-two and perhaps already worrying about being 'left on the shelf' and at a time when Thomas and Alice's marriage was on the brink of break up, Harold 'The Major' Melville arrived on the scene.

A dinner guest of Thomas Briggs at the family home, which was then in East Greenwich, Harold at twenty-five cut a dashing figure, lightening the gloom of a home no longer happy. And his presence and personality would for Berenice have possibly offered a way out of a life that was overshadowed by Alice's grief over Helen and her unhappy marriage to Thomas. Perhaps it was a sign of the times Berenice lived in, that like her sister Helen it took marriage to bring meaning and focus to her young life.

It has been said that Berenice was a free spirit. That's easy to deduce, because only a free spirit would have abandoned a life of wealth and ease to run off against all odds with a dashing Jamaican to what was for her an unknown island. I am sure that far from painting a picture of St Mary's mosquitoes or his rural home far from Kingston's bright lights and social life, Harold would have conjured up a magical tropical isle, warm weather year round, bright birds chirping in the trees with perhaps galas at the governor's grand official residence, King's House.

Glimpses of Berenice that give me a clue as to her character will come later when, during her life married to my grandfather Harold in Jamaica, my mysterious grandmother emerges like a butterfly from its chrysalis.

7

Meet 'The Major' and My Dad, John Melville

I knew from an early age that my dad's American grandfather, Thomas Briggs, had been an inventor, that he had become very wealthy, and that Dad, his siblings, and American cousins, Helen's three children, had inherited a fortune from Briggs's trust through Helen and Berenice. I thought of my own life, during which I had a mother and a father I took for granted, a home with us four boys who were relatively safe and nourished in a privileged life, protected by the legacy provided to us by the fact that my grandfather had married Berenice.

All that we had has shaped our life as a family, but the journey I took into my family's past would reveal at what price I enjoyed this tranquil life. That visit by Wally Parks to the Chukka Cove polo grounds would lead to my first glimpse of the Melville family story beyond the limited view and immediate life I'd known growing up with my father's generation and my own.

Wally Parks was as good as his word. It wasn't long before a brown envelope containing a copy of the promised chapter from his sister Lucille's book arrived in the mail at my office. I was not an enthusiastic reader in those days. When I did read, I read slowly and carefully. It's only now, being older with less temptation to do other things, I will settle with a good book, usually on history. I'm still slow as molasses. So when I brought the brown envelope back to Chukka Cove, it remained there for a few weekends before I became overcome with curiosity and opened it. It contained not only the chapter but also some research on the history of the Melville family that Wally had painstakingly explored. Before I get to the envelope's intriguing contents, however, let me tell you what I already knew about Harold 'Major' Melville.

Melville comes from the French 'de Malleville', a family that went to England with William the Conqueror in 1066 and was then granted lands and became a clan in Scotland. Some 700 years later, one Alexander Melville, born in Scotland in 1758, joined His Majesty's army in the American Revolutionary War of 1776 as a surgeon's mate. He saw active service until he was taken prisoner with General Burgoyne, who surrendered at the Battles of Saratoga. Melville was probably granted release in a prisoner exchange on Staten Island in 1781, before the peace of 1783. In 1786, he ended up on the Caribbean island of St Vincent as an ordnance surgeon with the British troops.

Alexander Melville was Major's great-great-grandfather. Alexander practised medicine in St Vincent for forty-three years until his death in 1829. He would marry twice. His second wife, Margaret Cox, produced seven children. To me, it's an amusing detail of trivia that, five generations after Alexander fought for the Royalists against the Republicans in the war that created the United States of America, Harold would travel from British colonial Jamaica to the US and take a bride from a family that claims lineage to the *Mayflower* and many of the oldest families in New England. That's karma.

Carole and I visited St Vincent in January 2019 and found this tribute to Margaret on a marble tablet in the nave of the south wall of St George's Cathedral in Kingstown, the capital. It reads:

A filial tribute to the memory of
MARGARET JANE MELVILLE
wife of Alexander Melville M.D.:
and daughter of HP Cox and Jane his wife:
who died on the 10th day of May 1829.
Aged 54 years.
She was zealous in the performance of her religious duties,
strictly virtuous and dutiful to her husband,
an affectionate and tender mother to her children,
firmly attached to her relatives and friends,
a most indulgent mistress to her servants,
compassionate to all in sickness or distress,
benevolent to those she found poor and needy,
to no one an enemy,
to everyone a friend.

I felt like I was 'home' and choked up a bit when I read the tablet as St Vincent is the cradle of my family in the West Indies.

Margaret's first child, Thomas, worked for a while in Barbados then ended up as treasurer of St Vincent until he died in 1841. For whatever reason, I dreaded the day I would find proof that my ancestors were slave masters at some point, but I knew it was inevitable the minute I undertook the task of writing this book. So I wasn't very surprised when our research revealed that in February 1836, Alexander and Margaret's firstborn, Thomas Melville (Harold's great-grandfather) and his wife Rebecca both received compensation for slaves. Because it was for only a few, this would indicate their slaves were probably domestic servants. Thomas received £58 15s 6d (approximately £3,551.01 in today's currency) for two of the enslaved while Rebecca received £117 11s 1d (approximately £7,102.27 in today's currency) for four. I never fully understood how it was that the slave owners were compensated for the 'loss' of their slaves, rather than the slaves being the ones paid reparation for the injustice they had endured.

So how did the Melvilles end up in Jamaica? Harold's grandfather, James Chapman Melville, was Thomas's third son. He was born in St Vincent in 1826. He emigrated to Jamaica as a young man in 1850 and within a year of arriving he married Mary Archer who was born in St Ann parish in 1831. He would make his mark and have a distinguished career as a planter's attorney representing various merchants and proprietors in England. He was a magistrate and a member of the Kingston Municipal Board where he sat on various committees that dealt with the management of the city. He also sat on several boards including the Standard Life Assurance Company and was at one time the Custos of St Thomas.

He donated land and built a church in Gayle, St Mary, where he lived. In 1870 he invested in and was on the management committee of *The Queen's Newspaper*, 'A monthly newspaper, specially designed for circulation among the peasantry of Jamaica'. He managed numerous plantations for absentee owners in England and he owned several himself. An upstanding citizen, he was known to give his time and money to charity including the Sailor's Home in Kingston, where he served as director.

The multitude of *Gleaner* ads, articles and notices, give us an idea of his business, buying and selling of properties and supplies for plantations; boiler tubes; 'a good and steady ploughman at liberal wages'; mules; a six-horse single plough; and a hundred more. And in the poor taste typical of the time, a racist ad selling a property, after listing the acreage, buildings and livestock, comes…. 'A fine lot of Coolies located in comfortable cottages!' This reflects the post-emancipation labour situation in Jamaica, where basically the former enslaved Africans who refused to work for their old masters had been replaced by indentured labourers from India who with typical British scorn were described as 'Coolies', which became a highly charged slur.

James and Mary had eight children. He and his wife travelled to England regularly on business, and two of their children were born there. He would become a wealthy man, but unfortunately, as did many others at that time, he was tempted to go into sugar and crashed with the industry. He owned several estates in the parish of St Mary, and when sugar declined, he lost most of that wealth. His eulogy in the *Daily Gleaner* in July 1901 reflects the high esteem in which he was held:

The Late Hon. J. C. Melville.

Another of our links with the past has been removed from our midst in the person of the Hon. J. C. Melville, who died at his residence on the Hope Road Saint Andrew, and whose remains were interred at the Halfway Tree Parish Church on Wednesday afternoon.

Mr. Melville was a native of Saint Vincent and came to this island as a young man about 50 years ago. He was largely interested in the sugar industry, and was the attorney for a large number of properties. He was too some time Custos of the parish of St. Thomas, where he had large interests in several sugar estates. Mr Melville also owned property in St. Mary and resided at "Gayle" until the death of his wife, when he came back to St. Andrew to live.

Mr. Melville was perhaps best known among Churchmen. A staunch Episcopalian, he took the greatest interest in the work of the Church and aided in directing its policy on the governing boards. He was the first chairman of the Diocesan Board after the disestablishment of the Church, and was for many years the treasurer of the Home and Foreign

Missionary Society. A modest and retiring man by disposition, only those who came into close personal contact with him could appreciate his worth and the good service he rendered to the Church. Mr Melville was a member of the Synod, and attended the last session, when he took active part in most of the business.

Mr. Melville was 75 years of age at the time of his death, and leaves three sons and two daughters. His illness was of short duration, as up to about a week ago he was apparently in the best of health. At the meeting of the Diocesan Council yesterday afternoon, a resolution of condolence was passed in respect to his memory.

I had no idea James was such an influential person in Jamaica. But there was one particular reference that struck a familiar chord; in January 1875 he applied to the Governor for Letters Patent for 'an improved method of evaporating and concentrating cane juice and other liquids'. So, my great-great-grandpa James was an inventor like my great-grandpa Thomas Briggs. If James was indeed 'a modest and retiring man' he was the polar opposite to his grandson Harold. It also appeared that unlike Harold he had great empathy for the downtrodden.

James Melville's sixth child was Lewis Brodie Melville, my great-grandfather, who married Louisa Silvera in 1886, and in 1887 their first born was a son they named Harold Archer Melville, my grandfather. His middle name was Archer after his grandmother. Four of Berenice and Harold's five children were given the Archer name and it has continued to this day. Uncle Tom was born in Rhode Island and was given the middle name Briggs after his American grandfather.

Lewis was not successful like his dad. After marrying Louisa, they lived at her family's farm, Crescent, in St Mary, where Harold and sibling George were born. Then they lived at Belleville also in St Mary, where John was born. Lewis Melville was a 'Busha,' the local term for the big man, overseer on a plantation. He inherited no plantations; he sold retail spirits, became a shopkeeper, then was the overseer of a large banana plantation at Whitehall owned by the Atlantic Fruit Company, another American-owned company involved in the banana export trade.

There's a fair bit about Lewis but mostly to do with horses and agricultural shows. Match racing – two-horse race usually run on a private estate road – was hugely popular back then; you can bet that's where Major got hooked on racing. Lewis was obviously an excellent horseman; there are several reports about him winning at agricultural shows in various parishes, even with driving horse teams. So, that's where Harold's love of horses came from, and then Dad's, then mine, and my boys: five generations of horse lovers.

There is a reference to a Lieutenant Melville in the militia in St Mary in 1904, but I can't swear it is Lewis. Is that where Major got the idea of playing soldier when he returned with Berenice from America in 1912? He was a volunteer in the militia, something that took up a lot of his time, and he was not a rich man. So, what was his motive?

Harold's mother, Louisa, was a member of the large Silvera clan who settled in Jamaica as part of a migration of Jews who had fled Portugal's Inquisition in 1530 to live in the new world, forty years after Columbus had landed on Jamaica's shores. I wonder if Harold felt that he had been cheated out of his grandfather's wealth, and that his lasting good reputation planted an expectation of him. Perhaps when he met Berenice, as he swept her off her feet with his sweet Jamaica lyrics, he saw her as his meal ticket to the life he felt he should have had.

Whatever sweetness Wally Parks may have intuited in Harold was probably due to Louisa's unmarried sister, Luna. Luna adored her nephew and took him under her wing. She practically adopted him, and when she went to live in New York City when Harold was a young man, she took him along with her. Being Jewish, she chose to live in Harlem. There, Harold would realize for the first time what it meant to be Jewish in America in 1907, to feel the sting of racial prejudice and not to have the social privilege to which he was accustomed.

Wally Parks's research expanded my background knowledge a great deal, filling in blanks and adding a much wider view of the various branches. But what really stunned me, when I finally read it, was the chapter about my grandfather Harold in the book by Wally's sister, Lucille Iremonger. The photocopied chapter taken from her memoir was titled simply *The Major*. Ironically, its pages were held together with a simple staple. I smiled.

Apart from some name changes – the writer changed the name Melville to Fairfax, no doubt to protect the guilty! – every detail about the five children was there. Those children include my father and his siblings, left motherless by the untimely death of their mother, my grandmother Berenice. Lucille's chapter about my grandfather focused on his life after my grandmother died in 1930, and this portrait of him was fascinating. It was a picture of a maverick figure, brash, persuasive, and commanding. Talk about life imitating art. I would find out later how true to life her story turned out to be.

Lucille, who is some thirty-two years my senior, had gotten to know the grandfather I never knew through her mother, who had been mesmerized by Harold. She describes the first time she met him, when she, her siblings, and mother and father visited him and his newly motherless children, including my father, in his home. The Major rose from his chair, appearing to her, a child, to be a giant figure, an enormous and imposing man 'almost ten feet tall' as he established his presence before them. She describes the huge torso of this looming figure, a man with a mane of thick steel-grey hair who kept pulling his belt up over his huge paunch. And although she remembers finding his charm compelling, she was aware that her father didn't. Lucille thought at the time that the title Major suited him, imagining him as a veteran of many successful battles, a true warrior, according to his boasts. However, her father dismissed the Major as a 'paper soldier', his military service only temporary, and disapproved of him keeping the title.

Lucille brings to life my grandfather better than any other description I've heard. I can see the imposing figure as he unfolds from his chair, a dilettante who, far from serving in noble battles, had enjoyed a life of generous indulgence afforded him by his marriage to my heiress grandmother, Berenice. Lucille refers to the irony of the Major living so comfortably from the profits made from such things as staple machines since he was 'the most unbusinesslike and unmethodical of men'. This disorganized person whose desk she describes as always a mess and who only opened letters that he knew would give him pleasure was sitting on his widow's fortune, using it to apparently live the 'life of Riley', and to sweep Lucille Iremonger's family into the chaotic realm of his hedonism.

This home Lucille visited with her parents and her siblings was obviously Courtville at Half-Way-Tree in Kingston. It was the place where my father and his siblings had grown up. She describes it as the great Elizabethan hall of the former courthouse from which the original benches and tables for the public and the press were removed; the bare floor that once held the witness box and prisoner dock now standing eerily empty and unadorned; the small rooms off the hall that once provided offices for the law clerks now replaced by a large dining table, six shabby wicker chairs, a piano, and a sofa. Although in the book Lucille describes it as the old courthouse, I think it was probably across the road from the courthouse but of similar size and style. Lucille may have seen the inside of the courthouse. I suspect there's a touch of poetic licence there.

Courtville was bought in 1928 and the family moved in that same year. Berenice's death two years later would leave their five children motherless. That was when the Major invited his cousin, a horse trainer, to move in with his seamstress wife – Owen and Angel Silvera – and an American governess named Miss Raab. He promptly started spending big money on his horses. The names are changed, but I recognized all the characters in the book; it was accurate to a fault. I had heard these details about my family in snippets over the years.

When I read Lucille's description of their visit to Major's house that day, I could picture these groups of children from two different families standing in what the author describes as a 'barracky existence': "They stared at us as enquiringly as we did at them." My father and his siblings huddled forlornly together, the boys in jodhpurs, as though as unused to outside company as the writer was, in this sparse home with a strange new caregiver and obviously a chaotic life. "We stood and looked at each other, pawns in a new, unknown game the grown-ups were playing."

Thanks to Lucille's writings, I was now seeing my calm and gentle father who I took for granted as the family's rock, in a completely new role and light. Every word in Lucille's chapter evoked for me the quiet image of a man I never heard talk about his youth, which now I found myself reading about. I thought about the effect my grandfather had on Lucille's unsuspecting family.

Along comes this charismatic man who, with ruthless indifference to the feelings of all involved, charms and bamboozles his way into their lives, their home, and her mother's heart.

My father, John, himself a devoted husband and father, had always been financially safe because of his mother's money. He never spoke of his childhood or losing Berenice at fifteen; he never spoke of his parents, showed no sign of having joyful memories. I'm not usually given to introspection, but I started thinking about my own youth growing up with my parents. And something that struck me was the presence of two photographs in our living room at Arthur's Seat.

It was a handsome room lined with St Ann yakka wood panelling, comfy sofas, and overstuffed chairs. There was a fireplace, for it got chilly in the winter months. In a dark corner near the fireplace hung the only photograph of my grandmother, Berenice, in an oval gilded frame. Probably taken when she was in her late teens or very early 20s, she is presented in profile wearing a large very fashionable hat that partly covers her face. She is beautiful. My mother had a small photograph of John's father on her dressing table, perhaps in deference to my dad. I didn't question my father back then about why there was no picture of my grandparents together; after all, most families have albums of their parents, wedding pictures, why not my family?

Hanging close by was the official 'corporate' photo of my great-grandfather Thomas Briggs, Berenice's father, and if one goes to the Bostitch website to this day, 120-something years later, you will see the same photo of the founder of that American company that became a household name. Growing up we knew who the father and daughter in the photographs were, but no one ever talked about them.

Yes, my life growing up was tranquil. My earliest memories are at Arthur's Seat; I was too young to remember living in Kingston. My father had bought the property, a 500-acre farm that sat 1,800 feet above sea level in the limestone hills of St Ann and moved the family there in 1952. This was a mountain home with beautiful sea views, and like many old Jamaican houses, it was surrounded by barbecues for pimento (allspice) drying. My father converted a large water storage tank into a swimming pool, and we had a rumpus room with an impressive American Flyer model railroad. The kitchen was a masterpiece of Jamaican tradition where our cook, 'Cookie', hung orange peels to dry near the wood stove; the best fire starter ever when dry. In the older and more historic part of the main house was the formal living room and nearby the dining room dominated by a solid mahogany dining table with twelve Windsor chairs. The house was tastefully updated over the years with the addition of long verandahs on two sides of the house and a modern kitchen.

By strange coincidence, Arthur's Seat had once been the holiday home of the Manleys. Norman and his wife, Edna would bring the boys down for the long summer holidays. I was able to show Rachel where her father and uncle's names had been scratched into the basement walls when her uncle, Douglas, and her father Michael were boys.

Moving there must have been a culture shock for my eldest brother, then fourteen, being uprooted from the big city of Kingston more than two hours' drive away in those days to the 'bush' of St Ann, with its dirt roads and no telephones. Our mail was delivered to the little post office in the village of Epworth less than a mile away, and if you needed to send a telegram you had to drive six miles to the town of Claremont. This was rural life in Jamaica – 'country'.

Helen and Dana Lawrence
circa 1904

Marian Lawrence
circa 1917

Helen with children. L-R: Marian, Leonard and Robert
circa 1902

Robert Lawrence

Leonard Lawrence

My Dad after a birdshoot

The Gleaner, *11 February, 1924. Clay Pigeon Shoot, St Mary*
L-R: Mrs Roy Johnson, Mrs Roxburgh (hidden), Mrs Henry G. Delisser,
Carmen Delisser, Berenice Melville

Major and Tom
circa 1927

The Five Melville Children
Back row L-R: John, Thomas, Alice
Seated L-R: Douglas, Mary
circa 1927

The Hastings Family. L-R: My Mother, Cecil, Alice, Teddy, John with
my Grandmother Vida Jones Hastings
circa 1923

My parents on honeymoon in England in 1937. L-R: Unknown, Aunt Mabs
Hastings, my Mum, Aunt Polly Hastings, Dad and a Hastings relative.

John Melville *Janet Melville*

L-R: Bryan, Danny, Andrew and Christopher Melville, 1948

Ivy Parks and the Major
circa 1935

Harold Archer Melville
circa 1925

Officers of the Local Forces with Governor Stubbs (centre).
Seated in front row, far right is my grandfather Major Melville.
Daily Gleaner, *January 6, 1928*

My Dad, in his racing colours, being led in after winning a race.

Dad getting ready for a polo match

Robert and Lillian Lawrence

My Dad and his sister Alice

My Uncle Thomas Melville

L-R: Joseph Griffin, Aunt Alice and Dad in Holmdel, NJ

The land at Arthur's Seat was hilly and there was very little topsoil. I suspect my dad only bought it because although he wanted to move out of Kingston where he played polo at the Kingston Polo Club, sometimes at the Garrison Polo field at Up Park Camp, the British military camp, he wasn't prepared to lose access to his polo, and this farm was only seven miles from the St Ann Polo Club at Drax Hall Estate. This way he had the best of both worlds. Dad loved horses and shooting; those two sports were his life, and when he eventually gave up polo in later years all his energy went into shooting. I never thought about it then, but the two activities that gave him most pleasure he learned from his father Harold. So how come his dad wasn't his hero with a photo somewhere on his wall?

In those days the grooms rode one polo pony and led two others from the farm to the polo club every Saturday morning. Dad played polo in the afternoon, and while the club members imbibed and gossiped at the clubhouse into the night, the grooms rode horses back to the farm. Sometimes I'd get to ride home with them. It was cool riding at night and we'd stop at Connie's, a little rum bar in Steer Town for a quick one before riding the last four miles uphill to the farm.

Our farm, I understood later, operated as a tax write-off for Dad. He had a small herd of Red Poll beef cattle and stables where we kept about twenty horses, a dozen or more polo ponies, a few mares, and young stock. About one third of the property was woodland. Dad placed bending poles and cavaletti for basic training of the horses on a level common near the house.

For his other passion, he built a complete skeet and trap shooting range and, when home from boarding school, we spent hours on summer afternoons blasting away at clay pigeons. In the bird shooting season, which began on August 1 and lasted twelve weeks, my dad would wake us up before dawn to go dove hunting.

Dad loved his guns, but he was also a stickler for safety, going as far as stapling a huge Remington poster, 'The Ten Commandments of Gun Safety', on the back of our bedroom door. We were regularly drilled about gun safety. For obvious logistical reasons, one of the 'Ten Commandments' was never to climb through a fence with a loaded gun. That was how Harold's grandfather Lewis is said to have lost his life, supposedly climbing through a fence with a gun in pursuit of a mongoose. I discovered this was shortly after his maid had a baby for him, more reason perhaps to kill himself because he knew his society wife would have killed him when she found out!

My father was not a lazy man, up at the crack of dawn every day chopping wood and practising his swing with a polo mallet for exercise. He rode and schooled horses and drove the tractor on the farm. He had a tool room with every imaginable implement and did all the plumbing in the house and on the farm himself. But unlike the parents of my friends, who went out to work or to the office every day, my dad never had a 'job'. The farm made no money, but we lived very well from the cheque that arrived every quarter from the Rhode Island Hospital Trust in Providence.

Dad was also not a spendthrift. He counted his money carefully, literally squeezing every banknote when he counted them. He always liked to have cash on hand and had every denomination of note small to large held together with rubber bands. This money was kept in a little well-worn black leather briefcase that was his trademark. He only splurged on his two passions, shooting and polo. He dressed modestly and did not much care about fashion, though he did indulge my mother, who on the other hand spared no expense on clothes and make up, prompting people to refer to them as the beauty and the beast.

Every Friday of life was market day in St Ann's Bay, the parish capital ten miles from the farm. It was a ritual for my dad to drive the family in the car while the chauffeur would follow behind in the Land Rover Defender pick-up.

The tiny village of Epworth was pretty remote; the rural bus service stopped at the intersection at the foot of the hill and the villagers had to carry their belongings and walk uphill the last mile and a half. There were very few private taxis back then and if available were expensive to hire.

My dad developed a routine assisting the small farmers in the village by carrying their bags of cabbages, carrots, onions, escallion, and other vegetables in the pick-up to the St Ann's Bay farmers' market. Equally important, the couple of tiny shopkeepers in the village came to depend on this ride. Having purchased bags of flour, cornmeal, rice, and cases of salt-fish (dried salted cod), bully-beef (tinned corn beef), sardines, and such things from the wholesale stores in St Ann's Bay, the pick-up would haul the goods back up the hill to Epworth for resale in their little shops.

While my mum spent hours in the Hew's supermarket, I would stock up on Archie and Superman comics. My dad would in the meantime, with raw cash drawn from the bank for his payroll, visit the hardware store, the saddler (there was always a bridle or saddle in need of repair), and other farm related businesses.

Eventually everything, including supplies for the village shopkeepers, would be loaded into the trunk of the car and back of the pick-up, and the caravan of two overloaded vehicles would head for the hills and home to Arthur's Seat. That simple act of kindness was carried on for decades, and the local people who benefited never forgot. This easy and mutually sustaining coexistence would have been more possible in rural life than for those living in the city, and my father fell quite comfortably into the habit that reflected his natural and unpretentious generosity. Fast forward twenty-five years, I was no longer living in Epworth but seeking to represent the people of the constituency as their member of parliament, and a few of the older villagers reminded me of my father's kindness that I had long forgotten.

That was my tranquil youth. I guess my lack of curiosity, my disinterest to this point, reflected my complacency with a comfortable life. I lived blithely unaware as it all passed in one ear and out the other. And as far as that inheritance went, it was just a fact I knew, and whatever life this had provided for us was just life as I knew it, having never known anything else.

Drawn back from my reverie while reading Wally's papers, I was now exposed to a new and quite unexpected perspective. An entirely unrelated family – Wally and Lucille's – had been deeply affected by my grandfather. Perhaps my older brothers were more aware of what was going on within the family, but as the youngest, I was only vaguely aware that somewhere out there beyond my immediate family unit there was tension. But having read Lucille's chapter and catching a glimpse of this surprising new view, for the time being my grandfather Major Melville settled back down into the furthest corner of my consciousness and I to my life at Chukka. Although it offered a window into new insights on my paternal grandfather, at the time, almost thirty years ago now, I just found the whole incident of meeting Wally and then reading the chapter about Harold a bit bizarre. I was not ready to discover the missing pieces of the genetic puzzle that makes up 'me'. And there the Major would remain until a visit to Arlington where the ghost of Berenice, the other side of this our family equation, reached out several decades later to catch my attention in an equally serendipitous fashion.

In a subsequent letter in which I acknowledged receiving the chapter, I asked Wally if he thought Major was eccentric. His reply came: "As regards the Major, I did not find him eccentric. He was flamboyant and a man's man, a charmer of women. He kept my horse and gave me guns. A sportsman, maybe irresponsible and not a businessman, but a character."

Major was indeed a Jamaican macho man. Within the few lines of Wally's reply I sensed affection for Harold, but when I later found out more about Major, I had a hard time feeling any such affection for him.

8

The Elephant in the Room

Growing up, I wasn't aware of any particular distinctions made about Jews in Jamaica. They were white; they were usually professionals – doctors, lawyers – some were farmers or horse trainers such as my relatives, others successful businesspeople, some even went into politics. There was no particular stigma attached to being a Jew. Strange as it may seem, Jamaica is one place I can say with certainty that isn't anti-Semitic.

I don't remember what my brother Chris and I were talking about once back in our 20s, or why the subject of the Major came up, as we never spoke about him much in my family, but I remember him saying, "Don't you know Major's mother was a Jew?" He was talking about Louisa Silvera. Maybe I did know, as I knew we were related to the Silveras, but it never crossed my mind that they were Jewish, nor did it matter; in my mind they were Jamaicans, so his revelation to me went in one ear and out the other.

In recent years I have come to realize that my Melville cousins scattered across the globe had no idea of our Jewish heritage, and of course my American cousins from the Briggs side who were descendants of New England WASPs probably had no idea either. The Jewish factor has not been highlighted in my family history, and that's why I want to explore it in more detail. Knowing how prejudiced America was towards Jews back then, treating them as second-class citizens, I can't help wondering whether Major ever revealed the fact that he was half-Jewish to the classically WASP Alice and Thomas Briggs when he asked for their daughter's hand in marriage. That this brash Jamaican with a Scottish surname was coming to take their daughter away to some mosquito-infested British colony in the Caribbean was hurdle enough to surmount; can you imagine their reaction had they known that their would-be son-in-law was half-Jewish? Might that have been a bridge too far?

There is no point thinking that because Jamaica wasn't anti-Semitic, and being a Jew wasn't considered a big deal, that either Harold didn't know or thought it unimportant to mention his Jewish legacy to his prospective in-laws. Because the fact is, Major first sailed with his aunt Luna to live in New York City in 1907; Luna wanted her nephew to further his education. He would return to Jamaica in 1911 when Luna died, and it was in between those years he met Thomas Briggs and then Berenice.

The 1910 US census shows Luna's address as Lenox Ave, now also called Malcolm X Boulevard, and West 141st Street; that's Harlem. In those days the population of Harlem was only ten per cent black; the majority of Harlem residents back then were Jewish and Italian immigrants. By far the largest number of persons listed on the census page with Luna Silvera and Harold Melville were Jews from Russia. So Harold would have been aware of the local feelings against Jews as he lived in this New York enclave. And that meant he would certainly have known that meeting the well-established Thomas Briggs, and especially his WASP wife, Alice, there was more than one reason it might be wise to leave that genetic detail unmentioned.

What was Harlem like in those four or five years from 1907 when Major was there with his aunt Luna? Coming from rural St Mary, either from Whitehall Estate where his father was the overseer, or maybe living at Crescent with his aunt, Harlem had to be a culture shock for Major. In Harlem in 1907 there would have been hustle and bustle in the streets, horse-drawn carriages, and early automobiles; in 1908, the Model T Ford first appeared. There would have been street vendors with hand carts peddling bananas everywhere, some from Jamaica. Bananas were so popular with the working class that the peel littering the streets became a hazard for pedestrians and horses, the government ordering a fine or short jail sentence for those caught dropping them on the ground. Major was coming from a plantation where banana skins were precious fodder for the pigs.

On 141st Street there would have been four and five-story walk-up brownstone apartments. An apartment may have been two or three rooms; sometimes there was a communal kitchen. Every building had external fire escapes where tenants sometimes slept on the long hot summer nights. There were also rooftops on which tenants escaped the heat, immediately reminding me of The Drifters' familiar hit "Up on the Roof" from the 1950s. Maybe young Harold Melville had times when he felt homesick too, and the world there was "getting him down." He might have missed the rural fields of his youth where you could gallop a horse or mark a bird: "I get away from the hustlin' crowds. And all that rat race noise down in the streets."

This was not luxury living by any means. Harold would soon have come to realize the stigma attached to living in a place that was essentially a Jewish and Italian immigrant ghetto. If he had lived under the social privilege his colour secured him in his former Jamaican life, that privilege, only skin deep, was useless in Harlem, where blood told a different story. Now he would know how it felt to be on the other end of the social equation.

I am speculating about all of this, of course, because I was able to find very few concrete details of my grandfather's life at that time. I do know Harold enrolled in City College of New York, which had moved their campus to Harlem in 1907. The 1910 US census gives only the usual basic information: address, age, occupation. Under 'Trade or Profession', Major listed himself as a Draftsman; in the 'General Nature of Industry' section, he put down 'Structural Artist'.

Statistics that draw a picture of Harlem at the time. There'd been a Jewish community of only twelve people in Harlem in 1869 that grew to almost 200,000 by 1915, a few years after Harold and Luna arrived. Foreshadowing later resistance to the arrival of blacks, existing landowners tried to stop Jews from moving into the neighbourhood. Apartment rental signs on occasion declared in German, *"Keine Juden und Keine Hunde"* (No Jews and No Dogs). Major would have seen these signs. Italians began to arrive in Harlem a few years after the Jews. By 1900 there were 150,000 Italians in Harlem. Both groups moved mostly into East Harlem as this enclave welcomed the various waves of the unwanted.

And what about the Silvera family history? It intrigued me, so I set off on yet another red herring, researching the history of Jews in Jamaica. And where else to go than the keeper of all things pertinent to the Jews in Jamaica: their *de jure* and *de facto* archivist, Ainsley Henriques, himself a descendant of Sephardic Jews from Europe. It's fascinating and rich and very long, so I'll give the abridged version.

In Jamaica today there are only around 200 Jews, but at some point twenty per cent of Kingston's population were Portuguese and Spanish Sephardic Jews. In fact, Spanish Town, the island's first capital, was founded by Jews. In 1530, less than forty years after Christopher Columbus arrived in Jamaica, the first Jews landed in the island fleeing the Inquisition. The Jews would aid the British in their conquest of Jamaica, and under the British, Port Royal became home to a large Jewish community who lived alongside the privateers, some of whom were Jewish. They bore 'letters of marque' from England, really licensed to plunder in the Age of Sail, for operating against the Spanish. The Jews actually gave economic backing to the raids against the Spanish.

In 2008 an old Jewish cemetery was discovered on the outskirts of Kingston. Tombstones were found to have not only Hebrew writing, but displayed the skull and crossbones pirate symbols. My Silvera ancestors in Jamaica traded with those pirates. Adeline Silvera, a distant relative, gives an account of how the family arrived around 1530, fleeing the Spanish Inquisition that began in 1478:

> During the Inquisition, Don Silvera Blackthorn (the Silvera family crest was a blackthorn) sent his son George, to England, both for his safety and education, and a large amount of money was placed to his credit in the Bank of England. The Inquisitors captured the father, and when they found that his money was in England, out of their reach, they burned him at the stake.

The family ended up in Jamaica. Fast forward to the 1800s: records proving the Silvera family's descent from Don Silvera Blackthorn were burned in Jamaica's great Kingston fire of 1882. Apparently, if you could prove unclaimed moneys as belonging to your family, you could recover the sum from Chancery in the Bank of England. But because the cost of making a claim was 1,000 pounds sterling, Louisa's father, Captain Silvera 'got vexed' and dropped the matter, though the sum they were claiming was said to be eight million pounds sterling. The story may have some basis in fact, but I've also learned that the unproven story about 'money in chancery' is common to many family legends.

Jewish pirate ships that targeted the Spanish and Portuguese merchant galleons proudly displayed the names of ancient Jewish heroes, *Prophet Samuel, Queen Esther,* and *Shield of Abraham,* these having been bestowed on them by Jewish pirates of Jamaica. The most notable Jewish pirate of Jamaica was Moses Cohen Henriques, a direct ancestor of Ainsley. In 1628, accompanied by Piet Pieterszoon Hein, Moses led the successful capture of the Spanish treasure fleet, and went on to help the Dutch capture of northeast Brazil from Portugal.

Interestingly, there's a pirate connection to the original Silvera family in Jamaica. Here's more of Adeline's family legend:

> *In the time of the pirates, two Silvera brothers owned a dry goods store in Kingston, Jamaica. They frequently purchased plundered merchandise from the pirates in Port Royal. On one occasion, they purchased bales of cloth, and received (unexpectedly concealed within the bales), a large amount of gold and jewels.*
>
> *On realizing that the pirates had made a mistake, and there being no way to dispose of the wealth in Jamaica, they decided that the only solution was for one of them to leave Jamaica permanently with half of the wealth. The decision as to who would leave was made on a wager. Each brother placed a lump of new sugar (wet brown sugar) on the counter of the store. The winner was the brother whose sugar first attracted a fly.*
>
> *In due course, a fly landed on the sugar, one brother took the jewels and gold and migrated to Mexico. The other brother kept the cloth and the store.*

Antonio da Silveira (the original spelling), a minister of a Portuguese church living in Canada, gives the following accounting of the origin of the family:

> *The name Silveira is Portuguese. The family is related to the first Portuguese conquerors of the Iberian Peninsula in the 11th century. The first official register is Gonalo Vasques da Silveira in 1378. All the Jewish families in Portugal adopted names of trees because of the Inquisition.*

Like so many refugees of persecution or conflict from different races all over the world who migrated to our sometimes imperfect coexistence of black and white and yellow and various shades of brown with space freely given for any religion, Jamaica offered them safe haven, a fact that reflects our national motto: *Out of Many One People.*

Although my Silvera relatives may have traded with pirates long ago, perhaps some pirate genes have travelled down the generations to embed themselves in Major's personality! As I've said, he really was a prick, an opinion I'm sure you'll soon share. After all, if going after someone else's wealth, being mean-spirited, and having a hunger for adventure and a thirst for danger are typical pirate traits, then my grandfather came by them honestly.

9

Berenice and the Major

I've always wondered how the paths of the Major and my grandmother Berenice crossed, and it's likely I will never find the answer but cross they did, joining two very disparate legacies with ripple effects reaching far and wide and including me.

Harold would lose his Aunt Luna when she died in New York in 1911 when he was twenty-four years old. This was a blow, for Luna had acted as his mother since the loss of his own. She adored her nephew, who would have been at the mercy of an unloving stepmother without her. But he was no doubt comforted by his inheritance of his aunt's sizeable property in Jamaica. Though not a major plantation, Crescent Estate, his legacy, would give Harold a home and a start; boasting rights when he needed to cut a glamorous figure.

It's been said that Harold planned to become an architect, but he never realized this dream although he took a course in draughtsmanship, and he was smart enough to adapt to this new environment and get himself a decent job with the railroad in New York. We do not know how Harold met Thomas Briggs.

One theory is that Harold had befriended a man in New York who came from Providence, Rhode Island. Harold may have visited his friend there; maybe the friend knew Briggs, and somehow on this visit Harold crossed paths with the famous inventor. Rich and successful as he was, Thomas Briggs had, as we know, come from a simple rural life in Little Compton, Rhode Island. When Thomas came to cross paths with Harold, the industrialist might have seen in Harold qualities that reminded him of himself when he was young: those of a go-getter. Harold must certainly have been vibrant and smart enough to have grabbed the attention of Briggs, because Thomas invited him home for dinner.

It is not difficult to imagine Thomas's younger daughter, Berenice, at twenty being enchanted by this dashing Jamaican. Harold was tall, strong, and very handsome. Adored by his mother and then his aunt, he always had a way with the ladies. He would have painted a romantic picture for the Briggs family of his island as a paradise of white sand beaches and swaying palms, perhaps evoking in Berenice ideas of the privileged life of a plantation owner's wife, the social life of governors' houses, race meets, and tropical parties. Berenice had led a sheltered life, watched over by her humourless mother Alice who was said to be a nagging, critical woman, likely exacerbated by Helen's death six years earlier. It was probably not a happy home. Berenice would have been looking for a way out. And there it was, sitting right there at the dinner table!

I wish we knew more about the meeting and subsequent courtship, but we can only guess. What did they discuss? Alice's family were said to be direct descendants of the *Mayflower*, and here was this Jamaican whose distant relative had fought ironically in the Battles of Saratoga – whom she no doubt would have considered of no account – charming her young daughter. At least his future mother-in-law didn't know of his Jewish background, as it's unlikely he would have told her. You see, Alice Briggs's claim to fame was that her mother, Miranda Grant, was a distant cousin of Ulysses S. Grant, leading one to consider this: During the Civil War, anti-Semitism had been at its peak in America. There were tensions over race and immigration, and a great deal of economic rivalry between Jews and non-Jews. From both sides of the slavery issue Americans were accusing Jews of being disloyal war profiteers, driving Christians out of business and aiding and abetting each side's enemy. In 1862 General Ulysses S. Grant issued General Order No. 11, expelling all Jews from the areas under his command, which included western Tennessee, Mississippi, and parts of Kentucky. It was a decision that would haunt Grant for the rest of his life, especially a few years later when, running for president, he needed the Jewish vote. Despite this, he did win the presidency. So maybe it wouldn't have been prudent for Harold to mention these genes, Jamaican tolerance to Jews notwithstanding!

In May 1912 Major returned to the United States for two weeks accompanied by his father, Lewis. They probably had free passage as the ship was owned by The Atlantic Fruit Company where Lewis Melville worked. It was on this trip that Lewis was introduced to Thomas and Alice Briggs as Harold's future parents-in-law, and the marriage certificate was procured. Harold returned in October to marry Berenice.

What we do have, after months of searching, is that marriage certificate. It states that on Monday, October 14, 1912, Harold Archer Melville and Berenice Briggs were married in Warwick, Rhode Island. It was witnessed by Marian Lawrence, Berenice's niece – Helen's daughter – and her father Thomas Arnold Briggs. Harold Melville, a 25-year-old white Jamaican of Scottish and

Jewish descent had married the heiress to half of one of the largest fortunes in Rhode Island. And soon after, in the thrall of whatever romantic notion had drawn her to this man and the vision of his land, which maybe she imagined as paradise, Berenice sailed with her dashing husband for their new life in Jamaica.

Perhaps in a fateful sign of things to come, as they landed in Kingston on November 10, 1912, Jamaica was hit by what would now be considered a category 3 hurricane, the strongest in the Atlantic that year. It meandered slowly around the island, lashing out with winds and flood waters, killing people, demolishing buildings, bridges, railway lines, and crops, including a quarter of the island's banana plants. The damage was estimated at £1.5 million, a significant sum in those days.

The local newspapers recorded the couple's stay at the Grove Central Hotel in Mandeville. The charming old hotel must have seemed a quaint and romantic place for a honeymoon in this idyllic countryside, and the newly wed Mrs Melville was probably euphoric. She had married her knight in his dazzling white suit and pith helmet, a tall, suntanned and handsome suitor who had charmed his way into her father's attention and her heart. He had rescued her from the dour, nagging presence of her mother Alice, and the stultifying darkness of the house from which her father escaped as often as he could in his fast cars.

Now in her new land, would she feel free of the mud of sadness she'd been stuck in since Helen's death? She may have dwelled on the thoughts of poor Helen's children, like motherless foundlings, lurching through their father's house, now under the command of their new stepmother and former teacher Anna Mathewson, seeking a sense of home, of affection, and routine so far away back in Rhode Island. It would be a constant reminder of how death could deal a blow at any time to the shape of family. But Berenice was now ready to start her own.

And a beautiful start it must have been. The green knolls of Manchester lie at the centre of the island of Jamaica, and Mandeville has long been the favoured spot of English expatriates. Its lushly green but tailored beauty, its well laid-out town centre and gently sloping fields with low, neatly stacked stone walls were comfortingly reminiscent of the English countryside. Most of all the higher altitude usually ensured cooler weather, and if it rained a lot, the English would also be used to that. The charming homes and tidy gardens with year-round bright tropical blooms, even the lushly exuberant hydrangeas and cottage flowers due to the cool climate, I'm sure enchanted this new visitor from America. If Berenice spoke to locals at the small hotel where the couple stayed, or looked at posted announcements on the board at the front desk, she would discover many events, including local plays and theatre groups, art exhibitions, and craft or writing classes attended by a cultured community.

Though none of her work still exists, we do know that Berenice was an avid gardener and liked to paint. My Aunt Mary remembers growing up with a huge still life of vibrant flowers that hung in her home painted by her mother. Mandeville drew many an artist to work because of its beautiful surroundings. What a feast of sunlight and flora Berenice would then have encountered for her first impression of Jamaica.

No doubt Harold, a charming fox, plied his young wife with exotic rum punches and romance, perhaps danced with her to some small local combo on the hotel patio under a tropical sky with its stars fiercer and nearer than up north, its moon strangely more intimate here.

The honeymoon over, Major whisked his young bride off to her new home in the low green hills of St Mary, a parish in the northeast of Jamaica. Now it was her turn to feel culture shock. Crescent was a modest property, only partly owned by Harold along with other members of his family – his mother's side, the Silvera tribe – but the main house was left solely to him by his Aunt Luna. By comparison to Mandeville, St Mary would have seemed far more rural and undeveloped. Much of its placid coastline was fed by rivers and powerful, breathtaking waterfalls.

Although Crescent was not near the coast, we know Berenice was adventurous and loved to paint, and there was much to inspire in the parish of the wild nature of this island, named Xaymaca by the Taínos, which translates as 'Isle of Springs'. From the majestically towering Tacky Falls named after a rebel leader, to the almost inaccessible but astonishing Kwame Falls named after Tacky's soldier.

Many of St Mary's landmarks are evidence of a fascinating history. Firefly Estate near Port Maria, was the home of the pirate Henry Morgan. It was later owned by the renowned English playwright Noël Coward who is buried there on the edge of the hill with the spectacular view of the Caribbean Sea as far as Port Antonio. St Mary is also the parish of the Rio Nuevo Battle Site once the scene of the watershed battle between the Spanish and British on June 17, 1658. Spain's inability to recapture Jamaica cemented the island's history as a British colony for the next 300 years.

So much beauty, so much history in every corner of this new land. But it's unlikely that Berenice got much opportunity to visit many of the beauty spots of her new home, living as she was on the farm. Also, she became pregnant almost immediately after they arrived at Crescent and was inundated with children thereafter.

Jamaica was still a full colony in 1912, when Berenice and Harold married, and wouldn't achieve its independence for another fifty years. So Berenice would have entered this privileged society, short on conscience or introspection, probably a class that would celebrate the defeat of the Spanish and its landmarks but might have been oblivious or insensitive to the island's deep history of pain or the heroic stories of its slaves. A waterfall would be something to be painted by a curious expatriate painter but probably not by a local plantation owner whose forays into forests would probably have been to shoot birds in the killing season.

Harold had owned horses from the time he brought my grandmother from America to live at Crescent. Back then I guess everyone rode horses, but being a very large man, it was unlikely that he played polo. I suspect that Berenice, coming from comparatively reticent New England and a small, quiet family, would soon have felt overwhelmed by the sheer number of people going in and out of her home, what with household staff, and family members dropping in. Perhaps she had morning sickness and dreaded feeling invaded, or did she feel grateful for the solace and diversion of their company?

St Mary was almost totally in the banana business by 1900. Crescent was mainly a banana estate in those days, busy with year-round farm workers, with some cattle, though later Harold would own two dairies in Kingston, Belvedere, and Pembroke Hall. Sugar had declined in mid-1800 and bananas had overtaken sugar as the main export crop. Harold's grandfather, James Chapman Melville had lost a lot of money on sugar in St Mary. And in another interesting twist, my mother's father, Norman Hastings, who had worked at the United Fruit Company, maybe bought bananas from Crescent for export? Major's father Lewis worked for the Atlantic Fruit Company.

What different surroundings these were for Berenice compared to her Rhode Island home. Farms bring swarms of flies in the day and mosquitoes after dusk; the rustle of rats in underbrush is a reality. Jamaica's nights are so very dark as the tropical sun suddenly drops behind the horizon. The chirping of crickets and tree frogs is relentless, as is the buzz of mosquitoes despite the ceiling fan, and the glimpses of 'peenie-wallies' – fireflies – like points of danger in feudal dark. How long would romance have mitigated the sense of strangeness here?

We know that Berenice's first child, Thomas, was conceived during their first month at Crescent as he was born in America on August 14, 1913, the year after her arrival on November 10, 1912. No doubt those early days were spent adjusting to her new environment, as she was probably unwell at first with morning sickness. By the end of March 1913, when she was approximately four months pregnant, Berenice's parents made their first voyage to Jamaica. Did Thomas and Alice Briggs come for a holiday or was this a rescue mission prompted by something Berenice had written in her letters? On seeing the circumstances of her life, did they persuade their only surviving daughter to return, if only just to give birth safely?

Whatever the reason, they set off with their daughter on the *Admiral Dewey,* which sailed from the port of Bowden in eastern Jamaica to Philadelphia, arriving on March 26, 1913. Nothing has survived to give us a hint of why they took the voyage, or who made the decisions. My uncle Tom was born in Providence, Rhode Island, on August 14, 1913, and Berenice subsequently returned to Jamaica. Was it her intention all along to return? Or had she meant to leave Jamaica and her marriage permanently but Harold persuaded her to come back? What were her parents' wishes? But return she did with her infant son to live again at Crescent with Harold. This would be Berenice's first of many trips home to see her parents, each absence leaving Harold with even more opportunity to get up to his mischief.

And he certainly did. I wonder at what stage my grandmother became aware of her husband's philandering. When she left on that first trip back to the US, was she already feeling abandoned by her faithless husband whose other woman probably lived on or near the property? Did Berenice know anything about it; had she figured things out? Did she sense gossip around her? She had to, I think, maybe not at first because she was away for a long time before returning home. What we do know is that in the same year Tom was born, 1913, Harold fathered another son, Keith, by one Josephine Silvera. At that time, Keith would be legally considered the illegitimate son of Harold. He could well have been conceived while Berenice was away.

Being a Silvera, Josephine was certainly related in some way to Harold, probably a cousin by blood. As far as I know the huge clan of St Mary Silveras were all related to each other in one way or the other and lived on or near the Crescent property. She was a dark-skinned beauty who Harold would have known long before he met Berenice. We don't know when their intimacy began, but Harold's extra-marital relationship with her was contiguous to his marriage.

I've tried to imagine my grandmother in her new landscape, and have attempted without success to retrieve, from the small image I have seen of her, anything that tells me who she was – even her smile, or the expression in her eyes. But I've been frustrated. Just who was she? And where are the family photos? Why didn't I demand to know more about her when there were people close to me still alive who could have answered my questions?

Some answers came recently thanks to my surviving aunt and cousins; these I cling to with an 'aha!' moment of excitement, analysing the fleeting impressions they offer. I have two cousins called Berenice, both named for their grandmother. My aunt Alice's Berenice I call Tahiti Berenice because that's where she lives, and Aunt Mary's I call Aussie Berenice for the same reason. Tahiti Berenice shared with me that my grandmother used to wear a red dressing gown and told fortunes, and that's why "my mother didn't like me doing the cards." She recalls that:

> *Berenice Melville I believe was definitely a free spirit like my Mum and most of the women in the family...liked being home but also liked going out for a party, adventure, new ways, new thoughts, travel. Berenice also shocked Jamaican society when she came back after a visit to Rhode Island and had cut her hair short; so she was a bit of a trend setter. Why would she have left Rhode Island to go to Jamaica...? Imagine a tall, tanned, smooth-talking, laughing, charming man coming into a stuffy English/ American society where everyone was trying to be something else other than themselves ...don't forget men are led by their eyes...women are led by their ears... and yes she more than likely enjoyed good sex! It's in the genes! She chose freedom and adventure!"*

And my other cousin, Aussie Berenice, gave an interesting picture of why her grandmother would have moved to Jamaica with Harold:

> *As to the marriage, well I also was told her father was furious that she "ran off" with grandfather, only to be "called home" often. I gather Harold was very charismatic and probably swept her off her feet with tales of the tropics and maybe as a girl she was taken aback by his status and the "small town" society? Or am I being too romantic? I know that in the early 1900s ... women of families of a certain standing were grudgingly allowed to be nurses or teachers but were more likely kept at home learning "how to run a household" until married off to a suitable gent. Very few were*

able to break the mould and often had to escape to far off places. It would be so interesting to find out.

Other than these few snippets that tell me Berenice was a character and perhaps a bit of a rebel, my grandmother seems to have simply evaporated from history, leaving little evidence behind of her living years; how come? It's as though she 'disappeared'. There are only a few remaining images that we are certain are of her.

In fact, it is extraordinary that only one small full-face picture remains of Berenice, plus a profile, and a grainy picture in the newspaper. Not a letter. Not a sample of her handwriting. Not a trace. What do we know about Thomas's younger daughter whose wealth, virtually half of Thomas's fortune, would dominate so many people's lives in Jamaica and beyond? Very little. Three pictures, no stories. Berenice died young; she was only forty. Little Mary was not even seven years old at the time of her mother's death, Tom was seventeen, John, my dad, fifteen, Alice fourteen, and Douglas twelve. Presumably they remembered a lot but just didn't talk about the trauma of losing their mother. Apart from the odd glimpse I'd discover later on, it is as though she has become invisible. A voiceless ghost.

We don't know how Thomas and Alice Briggs felt about their daughter's return to Jamaica after giving birth to Thomas, nor do we know exactly when Berenice and baby Tom returned to Harold, but for better or worse Berenice returned and threw her considerable lot in with her Jamaican husband. If this heiress who was used to great luxury and comfort had initially found it hard to adjust to the comparative heat and simplicity of rural life in Jamaica, now she knew what she was returning to: all the things that went with a banana plantation with livestock, including the smells of manure and the presence of flies, mice, and rats. She had clearly decided to meet the now-known challenge.

Of most consequence for me, two years later, on November 20, 1915, their second son, my father John Archer Melville, arrived, born in Kingston. As this would have been Berenice's first delivery in Jamaica, Kingston with its superior medical facilities, was chosen over a St Mary home delivery. Meanwhile, Harold's second family was also growing. Harold and Josephine's second son, Vincent, would be born the same year as my father; the cheek of it! Harold and Josephine's third child, Seymour, was born in 1920.

It is difficult to assemble the pieces, to get a sense of the years between Berenice's arrival as Harold's wife and her first appearance in the *Daily Gleaner* on February 11, 1924: a report on an inaugural meeting of the St. Mary Sporting Club for a Clay Pigeon meet. Berenice is posing with a Mrs. Roy Johnson, Mrs. Roxburgh, Mrs. Henry Delisser, and Miss Carmen Delisser. These were the names of the island's plantocracy of the day. When I first saw this I must admit I felt my heart jump – my grandmother has arrived, I thought! She was taller than the other women, almost statuesque, with ramrod straight bearing. A true thoroughbred. Just a little heavy, perhaps, having by then just given birth to her fifth child.

And what was Major up to? His activities can be tracked through public record; at this stage they reflected farming and his new somewhat overblown military career in the West Indies Regiment, from which came his often-used title. The newspaper shows in 1914 that Harold attended the first agricultural show hosted by the Jamaica Agricultural Society at Moore Hall Common, where he entered his brown stallion 'Dutch Park', providing an early glimpse of what would become a lifelong love of horses. From December 1915, references to the Major are mostly as a soldier of the volunteer army at the Jamaica War Contingent Camp where he was transferred from Platoon 8 as Vice Lieutenant to take command over E Company. In 1916 the *Daily Gleaner* reports on January 3 that "Lieut. H.A. Melville of the Jamaica Corps of Scouts was transferred as Lieutenant to the Jamaica Reserve Regiment for service with the third Jamaica contingent of the British West Indies Regiment." In August that year he is listed in *Who's Who Jamaica* on the Reserve List of the Local Defence Force on the Jamaica Corps of Scouts. Similar regimental announcements are reflected in the *Daily Gleaner* in 1917, and by June that year he is appointed as a Second Lieutenant of the Jamaica Militia Artillery. This is not surprising to me as we know that my grandfather, an avid bird and skeet shooter, loved guns.

Also in 1916 we learn of Harold's offer through the Agricultural Society to the Custos to provide his services to become a Justice of the Peace (JP) for the area. In the English colonial system the prestigious Custos and the lowlier JP, though not paid positions, had certain administrative duties that added an air of authority, bearing the stamp of approval of the English Governor.

During this time, Harold also became notably litigious and spent a lot of time and money fighting various lawsuits with varying outcomes. Unfortunately, most of the cases showed Harold as a bad egg: not paying his bills, or unreasonably suing people – sometimes humble people of great needs and little means. In 1916 comes the first of many notices of Harold Melville bringing various lawsuits. These were usually noted briefly in the newspapers with little explanation. In this initial instance he lost to Messrs. C.E. Johnston and Company for five pounds sterling, the price of goods sold and delivered to Harold, plus legal costs of one pound.

By 1917 there is a second lawsuit, this one against him. Mrs. Averil Duncan, a dressmaker, sued for payment of dresses she sewed for Berenice in which the defendant claimed that the bill was paid. I couldn't help thinking that it was one thing to be sued by a major company, but quite another to see my comparatively affluent grandfather in conflict with a humble seamstress. Surely, this didn't speak well of his reputation. One had to wonder how much disposable income Berenice had at this stage, or how much of her income was at Major's disposal – and also whether the Major told Berenice he had paid her bill when, in fact, he had pocketed the cash.

On March 23, 1917, the Melvilles' third child, a first daughter, Alice Archer Melville, was born at Crescent. Perhaps Berenice had found a good midwife? Berenice and Harold had had three children in just three-and-a-half years. And one wonders if Berenice knew that within this time period her husband had fathered two children with Josephine. It's interesting that both Josephine's children were given their father's surname which would suggest that Harold did take responsibility for them as his children because in those days if he didn't, their birth certificates would not have reflected the Melville name.

Given all this, how happy could life have been at home with Berenice? We know that she had become friends with Vera, the wife of Harold's cousin Owen Silvera. They were pregnant at the same time, company and a comfort for Berenice. But both women caught malaria. Berenice, who had just given birth to her third child, was expected to die, and Vera, still pregnant, was expected to live. But Vera died along with her unborn child. This loss must have been a blow for Berenice, but life went on. On November 21, 1918, Harold and Berenice's fourth child, Douglas Archer Melville was born, again at Crescent. In 1920 Major registered as a Lodge member with the United Grand Lodge of England Freemasons. In the same year he was elected as an associate member of the

American Society of Civil Engineers, and the following year was granted a commission as a land surveyor in Jamaica.

In the meantime, Harold and Josephine had a third child, Seymour Denzil Melville in 1920. Josephine was obviously no passing fancy for Harold; his emotions for her clearly rivalled those he owed to Berenice in his marriage. This leads me to wonder if he stayed with my grandmother for her money, or the hope of having it one day. Either way, Berenice's money must have provided the lifestyle they all enjoyed. Yes, even his outside family too.

In spite of all this, it does seem Major had a good public reputation. Although the Great War ended in 1918, in July 1921 there is an interesting notice in *The Daily Gleaner* about the army forces of Jamaica. It says that the island should guarantee its own defence in case of an emergency, and it states the conditions of service and duties of militia and volunteer units. The 'excellent services' of the Gunner Corps of the Jamaica Militia Artillery are lauded as efficient and of a high standard by inspecting officers. Lt. Melville is singled out as having served during this 'trying period' and would be remaining in the Corps 'ready at any moment once again to man the big guns in defense of the island'. By December it is reported that he has been promoted to Captain in the Jamaica Military Artillery Force.

Then comes the report of another lawsuit, also in December, this time in the St Thomas court in which an A.B. Francis claimed injuries to his mules and his cart caused by the defendant Harold Melville's motor car. After several adjournments, Harold counter-sued for damage to his car, and in July the following year the judge ruled in favour of the defendant on both counts. Harold had won the suit and the countersuit. Again I am left with the feeling of, if not injustice, then imbalance. A simple carter and his mule versus Harold and his motor car? It seems an unequal feud that surely

Harold could have resolved by simply helping a fellow human being of such limited means, seeing that his cart and mule was probably his only livelihood.

With all of these pieces of evidence, I was beginning to form a picture of my grandfather as a lucky but disloyal man of low morals and, worse still, a ruthless and uncaring cad of ungenerous heart, willing to use and betray his wife, and with no compunctions about using his power and means to crush those of more humble circumstances. It's not the kind of man one wants their grandfather to be.

By March 1922 domestic life with four children seemed to be taking its toll on Berenice, as an advertisement appears under 'Help Wanted' in the *Daily Gleaner* on March 11. Needed was 'a nurse, previous experience in caring for children essential'. Applications were requested to be sent to Mrs Melville. Berenice had sent out a call for domestic help.

There are two *Gleaner* announcements of note in 1923. One about Harold describing a presentation of war medals by the governor to the men of the Jamaica Military Artillery at the cenotaph for "guarding our island home, and principally our harbour, from invasion." Captain H.A. Melville was presented with the war service badge at Militia Headquarters. The second is a birth certificate on December 10, 1923, of the Melvilles' fifth child, Mary Archer Melville, born at Fontabelle in Trelawny. After nearly a five-year break between their fourth and fifth child, one can't help wondering if this birth was unexpected. This would be Berenice's last child.

They'd moved during that year from Crescent to a property situated to the northwest of Jamaica, east of Montego Bay in St James. Major was embarking on a new agricultural foray to plant sugar at a time when the sugar industry was collapsing worldwide. But what else was going on? Because shortly after this, they'd also sell the Trelawny property and acquire a farm in the Red Hills area of St Andrew, with the hopeful name of Belvedere: 'beautiful view'. Was he finally able to get her to spend her money?

I can only conjecture that Berenice embraced this latest move to the area north of Kingston as one that would free her from two things: her simple country life and her isolation within the Silvera clan at Crescent as an outsider. And maybe she had given her husband an ultimatum, demanding to be freed of her proximity to Josephine and her brood of competing Melville children. Maybe my grandmother hoped for a new start to her marriage.

10

The High Life in Kingston

I was surprised to discover that the Major went to London in 1924, leaving his wife with all five children, and the youngest, Mary, not even a year old. However, he went with Berenice's blessing. There may have been a plan afoot for the family to leave Jamaica, and this was when he went to investigate the possibility of a rubber plantation in Malaysia. I am sure that, given the fact that family is family and family news spreads, the Major would have been aware of the fate of the Brazilian rubber industry and the tangential involvement of his father's cousin, H.P.C. Melville. So surely he knew of the subsequent burgeoning industry in Malaysia. I can imagine Major the dreamer coming up with this crazy plan, what with the boom in car production around that time, and the rubber needed to manufacture tyres. But he came back from his trip less than enthused, having decided it made no sense. Better heads prevailed? He got talked out of it? Foreign plans sat in abeyance for a time, and life went on in Kingston.

Apart from jury duty for Harold in February 1925 – a ghastly domestic murder for which the husband was sentenced to death –

there isn't much about the Melvilles that caught the attention of the press. Berenice was now coping with a fifth infant, Mary, even if she did now have a nurse for assistance, and Harold was settling into the social life of Kingston.

Having moved to Kingston, it's difficult to know how much Harold was still able to see Josephine and his other children. Maybe Berenice hoped that at least the frequency of Harold's visits would be a thing of the past. It would seem that Harold continued his litigious ways as we see in the *Gleaner* in 1925, news of a car accident along the Spanish Town Road – the main road out of Kingston – involving Harold and Berenice Melville. Harold was overtaking another vehicle near an area where the public works had reason to dig a hole, which Harold claimed hadn't been properly filled in afterwards. In swerving to avoid it, Berenice was thrown out of the car, presumably uninjured, and Harold broke a rib and had to be treated in Kingston. Predictably, Harold put the matter in the hands of his solicitor, and a claim was made by November.

The Council claimed that the evidence showed Harold Melville was driving recklessly and ran into a trench. On investigation by the chief engineer it was revealed that the hole had indeed been properly 'crammed' and there was no open hole in the road. In an irony of fate, the barrister chosen to represent the city was none other than Norman Washington Manley, my friend Rachel's grandfather and the future Premier, who would be an influence in my youth forty years later. After preliminary hearings the city decided to defend the suit. This battle continued to the Supreme Court and is last mentioned in January 1926, though there is no mention of who finally wins. As N.W. Manley usually won his cases, I suspect Major may have lost this one too.

In 1926 Harold was promoted to the title of Major by the acting governor, and he attended several parades and practices, and a

Local Forces Rifle meeting, all showing how seriously Harold took his soldiering duties. He had apparently earned the title of Major that he would embrace ever after, even when his services were no longer needed. There are also mentions of plans prepared by him as a commissioned land surveyor, and even his attendance at a car gymkhana – a competition – at Knutsford Park Racecourse, which, given his propensity for fast and reckless driving, may have been worrying if not surprising. But of much more interest to me is the first high-society mention of my grandmother. The Major and Berenice attended the annual King's House Birthday Ball, hosted by the governor at King's House for the *crème de la crème* of Jamaican society. The Melvilles had arrived! This is the first of many such records of Berenice in the *Daily Gleaner* that covered all the important social events of the day. It is worth quoting the clipping from June 6, 1926:

> *Brilliant Function And Large Gathering Of Invited Guests. Perfect Harmony. Excellent Arrangements Made for Comfort and Entertainment of Company. The ball which was given by His Excellency Sir Edward Stubbs, K.C.M.G., and Lady Stubbs at King's House on Thursday in honour of His Majesty the King's birthday must rank amongst the most brilliant and successful functions held there. Invitations to be present were accepted by over seven hundred people and the majority were present... The guests who accepted the invitations, most of whom were present were...Major and Mrs. H.A. Melville...."*

Seven hundred guests! Things were hopping on the social scene in colonial Jamaica in the Roaring Twenties! To end 1926, on November 20 the Melvilles attended a 'delightful function held at King's House', described as 'The Governor and Lady Stubbs At Home'. And just six weeks later, on January 1, 1927, the Melvilles were again at King's House, this time for the Royal visit of the Duke and Duchess of York. 'Royalty Honours This Ancient Island

With A Visit' is the dramatically hyperbolic announcement from the *Gleaner*.

Berenice had mothered five children, with Mary now three years old, and in addition to what must have by then been a large household of staff, she had the help of a nurse at home. Perhaps whatever dullness and disappointment may have attended her years at Crescent in St Mary, this had now been replaced by the high life of colonial society in Kingston with her dashing Major. She had everything to live for. Later in January Berenice had a visit from her father Thomas Briggs. California's passenger records show that he boarded *The Fraconia* at Kingston Harbour bound for San Pedro, California.

Now based in Kingston, Major seemed to go into high gear as a farmer with his Belvedere property, proving himself if not always successful, certainly as daring as he was in everything else. On March 1 *The Gleaner* reports him at an auction sale of cattle at the Hope Farm buying a pedigree Brown Swiss cow for 18 pounds 10 shillings sterling, and Beryl, a grade Holstein dairy cow for 57 pounds 10 shillings. Two weeks later, he advertises for sale a four-year-old pedigree jersey bull 'In fine condition' and two high-grade Jersey Heifers, giving a Kingston postal address for applications. He advertises again a week later but lists his address as Belvedere.

In the next few months there are several mentions of his volunteer military career and in June, Harold and Berenice are once again at King's House for the King's Birthday Ball. Later that month, Berenice arrived in New York on the ship *Zapaca*. She doesn't appear to be accompanied by her children and she returned to Kingston on July 19 on the *SS Tivives*. She wouldn't have known that this trip would be the last time she'd spend with her beloved father. Thomas Briggs would die a year later, on September 24, 1928, and shortly after Berenice would be the beneficiary of her full inheritance – as opposed to receiving an allowance of some sort from her father, which had likely been the case thus far – through a complicated will left by her father that would have far-reaching consequences.

In August 1927, the *Daily Gleaner* describes yet another legal fight involving the Major, this one a right of way dispute, and again the nature of the suit reflects a certain small-heartedness and lack of public spirit in the Major:

> *Quite a number of residents here journeyed to Half-Way-Tree yesterday to hear the trial of a case which is (of) far reaching effect to the whole district. Some weeks ago Alpheus Follkes and two lads were arrested in connection with the taking down of a fence erected by the owner of Belvedere. From time immemorial there has always been a right of way through this particular part of Belvedere. Some years ago the late Major Prett tried unsuccessfully to stop people from using the track. Succeeding owners never interfered but Major H.A Melville, the present owner, wants to deny the people of what they claim as their rights, so he stretched a wire fence across the path which the people chopped down and in connection with which Follkes and the two lads were arrested. At the trial at Half-Way-Tree the case against Follkes was dismissed.*

The Major had lost! But of more significance is to understand the obvious indifference of Major to the realities of Jamaica as a colonial island in which there were a small number of privileged citizens like him, and a majority who lived in abject poverty, often without any transport but their own two legs. On an island with very basic infrastructure, a shortcut through someone's vast acreage could help children with miles to travel to get to school on time or domestic and other workers to be punctual. What kind of person would deny them that?

I try to weigh the paucity of facts to put the Major in perspective. Perhaps he just liked the excitement of litigation or maybe it made him feel important. And to his credit, he did recognize his outside children and seems to have supported that family in some fashion, albeit probably with Berenice's money. And what of Berenice's generosity? All these properties the Major was buying were no doubt paid for with her money. There is a story I would hear that will always haunt me. One of Major's grandchildren from the Josephine Silvera line described how her father, one of Major's sons, remembered being the little boy outside thinking of the grand lady of the house, Berenice, as a movie star from America and a disdainful snob. It could not have been easy for Berenice to be the wife of a philanderer, and by the same token neither could it have been for Major's illegitimate kids who were literally on the outside of their father's other opulent life looking in.

By August 1927 after many notices about the Major's service in the *Gleaner*, a clipping shows him being recognized at the Annual Militia Artillery Camp as a First Class Gunner, and throughout that year Major has played a leading role in many a military activity. There's even a picture of him with other officers and Governor Stubbs. On January 21, 1928, Stubbs visited the Red Hills and Rock Hall area of St Andrew, where Belvedere is located. He was there to 'see for himself the need for carrying out road improvements'. Many of the KSAC councillors, the municipality's governing body, were present as Stubbs officially opened a newly repaired Corporation Tank. The Major read a prepared address on the need for improved roads and water supply in the district. Berenice was present to lend her husband support.

The year 1928 would feature more military activity for the Major, and the resumption of Clay Pigeon Shoots at Wilson Park – Major is mentioned as one of Jamaica's crack shots. In June once again the couple is spotted at the annual Birthday Ball at King's House:

...a brilliant affair. Magnificent scenic effects served to emphasize the variegate spectacle. On the lawns surrounding the residence beneath electric illuminations of many kinds walked representatives of the church, the Army, the Navy, the Law, Medicine, the Public Service and Commerce, the uniforms and the beautiful and striking dresses worn making a gallant picture. The atmosphere was perfect and a beautiful big moon shed its light upon the scene...

Major Melville in his uniform would fit right into this scene so effusively described. These had to be the moments that made it all worthwhile for Berenice – the glamour, the attention, the sense of being the chosen who swim in the tiny goldfish bowl to the envy of all those who don't.

On September 24, 1928, tragedy struck. Thomas Briggs, Berenice's father, died. We do not know when she got the news, for communication in those days was slow and it might have taken days. And we hear nothing more about the Melvilles in the *Gleaner* until later in the year, when Berenice advertises on November 17, again for a nurse; in the ad she states, "No young girl need apply!" Indeed! She obviously knew about her husband's roving eye.

We will never know how lonely, sad, and disconnected Berenice felt learning of the loss of her father. Inheriting half of his fortune, Berenice became even more valuable to her husband. She was perhaps distracted shortly afterwards by the Major's brief foray into local politics; it was announced in a proclamation published in an Extraordinary Gazette that the governor had made arrangements for polling in the next election and that a determined effort was being made to get Major Melville to run in the St Andrew seat against Revd Gordon Hay. But whether through deference to his wife's grief or perhaps doubting he could win, the Major decided to withdraw. As for the remaining entries for 1928, they make no mention of Berenice, and the Major returns to his cattle farming and his military duty.

But thanks to her 'help wanted' ad in the paper in November, what we do know is that Berenice, who unfortunately would have only a couple of years left to live, very much knew her wayward husband. And when Thomas Briggs died, his will would reveal that possibly he, too, in the years of their association, had got to know the nature of his son-in-law.

11

Berenice's Death and Mary's Memories

I was surprised to learn from my aunt Mary, Berenice and Major's youngest child, that the family had planned to migrate to the US and that Berenice bought a property there in the summer of 1930, a few months before her death. I'd never heard about this move before, but it made total sense as Berenice now owned half of Bostitch through her dad's trust, and her children were getting older. Tom, the eldest, was seventeen, and his mother would have wanted him to go to college in the US, so having a base in New England would be convenient for her frequent visits there. This is pure speculation, but I'm sure the planned move would have been phased over time without completely cutting ties with Jamaica; otherwise why would Berenice have bought three properties in Kingston between 1928 and 1930? If there was any doubt about who paid for these properties, we find out years later from Major himself. The *Gleaner* reports in 1939 of the 'public examination' in the Supreme Court before the Hon. Mr. Justice Savary into 'the bankruptcy of Harold Archer Melville'. Major was reported as stating "Molynes was bought for me as a present by my wife in 1929." It was also reported that 'His wife bought a place at Half-Way-Tree for £1,600', this would be Courtville, and 'He owned a property called Pembroke Hall which was bought by his wife in 1930 and given to him'. Berenice bought him three properties in two years!

After Berenice died the cultural connection with America but not the monetary one, died with her, and except for Tom who was a US citizen, the other children were eventually shipped off to England to boarding school.

Major made a solo trip to New York on the *SS Santa Maria* in April 1929. He may have gone on business or to buy a car and ship it back to Jamaica, but we can't know for sure; he fancied large American station wagons and had one of the 'woodies', as they were called in those days. Much of what we have to go on regarding their lives is what's in the papers, and it's somewhat trivial. For example, while Major was away, Berenice was featured on the *Gleaner*'s local gossip page 'World and His Wife' as being present at the then-fashionable Bournemouth Baths. This was a favourite swimming haunt on the southern black-sand coast of Kingston which also had a huge salt-water pool. The Major was back in time for their attendance at the annual King's House Birthday Ball. For the rest of June and July 1929, Major busied himself with military gatherings. In August we see him at an agricultural show.

But there is a notice regarding the Melville family on September 30 of that year that is certainly not trivial. The headline reads, 'Mr. L.B. Melville Aims at Mongoose and Meets Death'. Lewis B. Melville, JP for St Mary and an overseer of the White Hall Estate banana plantation, was none other than Harold's father. He apparently shot himself accidentally when, seeing a mongoose in his garden, he ran to fetch his gun from the house. As he left with the weapon, he explained to his daughter Louise Melville, one of three children Lewis had with his second wife, that he was going out to shoot a mongoose. On hearing the shot she ran out to see if the creature had been killed, and instead was shocked to see her father lying there dead. The memorial was held the next day.

A mongoose is fast; it wouldn't wait around for Lewis's return and I also find it odd that he'd stop to tell his daughter about a mongoose he was trying to catch and kill outside. I may be wrong, but I suspect he wanted to give some explanation to his daughter before committing suicide. My hunch is based on hard evidence, too; after a lengthy enquiry that included several witnesses, the matter as published in the *Gleaner*, was thus resolved. Here is an excerpt of an exchange at the enquiry:

His Honour: From your observation is it more likely the wound was the result of an accident or is it more likely it was deliberately inflicted? What I mean is: Is the evidence more favourable to an accident or more favourable to a deliberate act?

The doctor: From all the circumstances either might have happened but from my observations I think it was more an accident.

This was clearly not a very convincing argument especially since we are told the insurance company subsequently refused to pay out on his policy.

Berenice and the Major had now both lost their fathers. I imagine this was more painful for Berenice who was close to hers. The Major had probably, as a young man, distanced himself from his father after he remarried, as he didn't get along with his stepmother. Major diligently continued his military duties. Not only did such prestige grant access to the governor, but I also believe in many ways this volunteer work more than anything else defined who the Major was in his own mind. On November 30, 1929, the *Gleaner*, reporting the end of the annual Militia Artillery Training, reports: '...very often Major Melville was the only officer at Rocky'.

For the remaining weeks of the year, and what would turn out to be Berenice's last Christmas season, the couple is seen celebrating the holidays at the fashionable Myrtle Bank Hotel in Kingston, where the Jamaica Scottish Society held its annual dinner. There were no bagpipes, but haggis arrived piping hot and was duly cut by the chairman. The Melvilles were feeling the holiday spirit and were seen several times at Bournemouth Baths, swimming and dancing, probably aware that due to their upcoming plans to emigrate this would be their last celebration of its kind here on the island.

The Major kept up his military duties in January and attended a lecture in February by a Dr Carley at Mr Watt's Dairy, St Andrew, stressing the value of clean milk for the people. He was accompanied by Berenice and 'the Misses Melville', young Alice and Mary, though Mary would have been only six years old. In March Harold and Berenice spent an enjoyable 'At Home' evening aboard the *HMS Durban* hosted by Captain Leatham.

It's around this time that the plan to leave Jamaica seems to have gained momentum. The family would take a trip to the US with all five children looking for a place to resettle in Berenice's home state of Rhode Island. They had no idea that in a few months Berenice would die. On April 10, 1930, Berenice, accompanied by Thomas (sixteen), John (fourteen), and Alice (thirteen), landed in New York on the *S.S. Santa Marta*. They were to be joined later by the Major with the other two children, Douglas and Mary, sailing on the same ship on May 3, 1930.

It was a major trip, and the family did some sightseeing when they were all finally together; there are records of Berenice and the whole family crossing from Canada via Buffalo into the US. It seems they visited Niagara Falls as a family. Thanks to this side trip, I learned for the first time the colour of my grandmother's eyes as on June 11, 1930, US Border Crossings records list Berenice Melville, Female, aged 40, arriving in Buffalo. 'Eyes blue'. My grandmother had blue eyes. For the record, mine are grey-green.

My aunt Mary says Berenice bought property in Rhode Island, and also visited East Greenwich, where Berenice grew up. I think they probably connected with Helen's children, their older cousins. This indeed had been a preparatory trip for migrating, maybe later that year or the next. On July 15, 1930, the *Gleaner* reports the return of Harold and Berenice and their five children on the *SS Santa Marta.*

But did Harold ever intend to leave Jamaica? Maybe not; for one thing, it appears that he may have been thinking of standing for election again as a councillor for the KSAC. According to a *Gleaner* report on July 8, he was asked to run, although that doesn't mean that was his intention, or, maybe he had told no one of the plans to migrate. I tend to believe this theory that Berenice, who had come into her full inheritance since her father's death, was buying the place in Rhode Island to take her children, and perhaps Major did not necessarily plan to cut all ties with Jamaica. It wasn't that unusual for families to divide this way as it would be the case for many families who split up in the 1970s, just like mine did.

There's no point speculating, for the last time we will hear of Berenice is in the *Daily Gleaner* on August 16, 1930, in its magazine's Special Features section, where she is seen with her children at the Bournemouth Baths. For me, there is something poignant about that report, knowing that within ten weeks Berenice would be dead, leaving these five children, like their cousins in America, motherless.

The story goes that Berenice got infected with typhoid in Mandeville. We are told that she caught the disease from a chambermaid at the very hotel where they spent their honeymoon as it was going around at the time. My grandmother was very ill for a while, but apparently she was on the road to recovery when it's rumoured the doctor made her have a couple of enemas. These caused her to haemorrhage and shortly after she died.

On November 1, the Jamaica Civil Registration provided the certificate of death from Kingston's St Joseph's Sanitarium stating that Berenice Briggs Melville's cause of death was 'Typhoid Fever', and it was signed by L.D. Moody. (Dr Ludlow Moody happened to be Norman Manley's brother-in-law.) And so, just like that – reminiscent of Helen's death – the mother of five children, one of whom was my father, was gone. She was just forty years old.

The death notice for Berenice appears in the *Daily Gleaner* November 5, 1930:

Melville – Berenice Briggs: Wife of Major Harold A. Melville on November 1st, 1930. Laid to rest at Half-Way-Tree Church Cemetery on Sunday morning. Rest in Peace.

The *Rhode Island Pendulum* would make its second and last mention of Berenice when it announced her death later in November when the news reached the East Greenwich Community. The first mention had been in 1908 when as a girl she had attended a church social. She 'was well known and had many friends', was how the paper described this long-lost daughter of America and its community. The article also fills in some details about her final trip with her family five months earlier in June, describing her as having recently visited her family, staying for a few weeks at the Greenwich Inn which still exists – it's now the

Greenwich Hotel and Lounge– sightseeing and visiting old friends before leaving on July 1 for a family vacation in Canada.

I often think about the irony of my grandmother's death, which came at the very moment when she was probably happiest. She was preparing to leave the island where she'd possibly felt humiliated for years by the coexistence of her husband's second family. This was a chance for a second start, a reinvention of their marriage, one that perhaps she thought would be on her own turf and therefore more on her own terms. She was now a wealthy woman and could live a comfortable life in her homeland with her family. Her husband could purchase a fine farm and fast horses, her children could attend the best schools – everything would be the way she likely hoped for. As she swam and played with her children at Bournemouth Baths, probably daydreaming of a new future, she would have had no idea that she was soon to reach the end of her journey at the nearby St Joseph's Sanitarium.

Mary, Berenice's last child, is the only sibling who remains alive today. As of 2020, she was ninety-six years old and living in Victoria, Canada. It is mainly through her incredible memories that I am able to form a picture of the impact of the loss of their mother and the shape of family life afterwards. And the innocence of those memories is perhaps best reflected in her recollection of Jamaica when she was growing up as 'a very peaceful place where everyone got along with everyone else and there was no animosity or discontent'. Animosity and discontent she only saw upon her return from England to visit after the Second World War, when she was faced with the start of riots in the streets of Jamaica led by National Hero Sir Alexander Bustamante. At that time Bustamante was a young trade unionist and would go on to become Jamaica's first prime minister in 1962. Island-wide unrest was at that time prompted by the sugar workers' strike at Frome Sugar Estate in 1938. Jamaica wasn't granted universal adult suffrage until 1944; before this, only landowners who paid property tax could vote. This 'discontent' she describes would have been part of the climate of change that Mary saw, as a people struggled for their empowerment.

Mary was almost seven years old when her mother died, but still sharp she remembers it clearly. Listening now, to the last surviving member of my father's siblings, and reading her letters that answered my questions about the past, one senses behind the memories a child whose entire life and routine were reshaped by her mother's death. Being the youngest, the baby girl of the family, she would cling to and defend her father, who became her vulnerable life's sole grip on security.

Mary has helped me to build a picture of their lives after Berenice's death. The family had sold Belvedere in the hills of St Andrew and recently purchased Courtville, number 9 Hagley Park Road in Kingston. This was in addition to the two others recently purchased, Pembroke Hall and Molynes Road farms. Mary describes Courtville as 'my mother and father's home'. They had moved in and alterations on the house were underway. They had removed a useless portion of the verandah from the side of the house and taken down a wall that had made the sitting and dining rooms very dark, and the house was still partially in a state of rubble when the tragedy struck. Any cynical suggestion that Berenice's money provided Major with his lavish lifestyle and the several recently acquired properties is swept aside with Mary's childhood memory of simply expressed faith in a predictable and traditional marital world where it's 'my mother and father's home'. There had been no doubt in her seven-year-old mind that it was her father's home just as much as it was her mother's, and one wonders if she has spent a lifetime defending her father against a poor impression others may have had of him as a philanderer and opportunist.

I don't think Mary has many memories before Courtville. She paints a picture of a world peopled with neighbours and friends. The Machados were close friends of Harold and Berenice; Benny Machado was a dentist and had gone to school with Harold, and Mrs Machado, his second wife who was English, was Berenice's closest friend. The Machados had four children. Benny and Berenice shared a keen interest in orchids. Then there was the Powell family, including four boys who lived across the road. They were also close friends of the family, but when the husband had a shipboard romance with a teacher coming to work in Jamaica, Mrs Powell left for England with the boys. Mary seemed to have kept in touch over the years.

Berenice seems to have made friends easily once she lived in Kingston and had access to a social life. Mary remembers being bundled often into the car, her father 'being a Major' they'd visit the army base where the colonel in charge was her father's good friend, and Berenice became friends with his wife.

Mary paints from her little girl memories a happy and normal if somewhat abundant family life for the kids – friends coming to tea, picnics on the grass at Bournemouth Baths, kids getting sunburnt. She remembers a full live-in staff of cook, gardener, laundress, butler, and driver.

At the time of her mother's death, Mary had begun attending a middle-class nursery school. During that period in Jamaica, many were run by spinsters working out of their homes like Miss Farquarson's, just up the road on Hagley Park Road. At school, Mary's best friend was the daughter of the famous Valentine's

Bakery family, an early institution in Jamaica, whose vans bearing the family name even I can remember. As for her siblings, Tom, John and Douglas went to Munro College, a boy's boarding school, at one point. Alice went to Hampton, a boarding school located in Malvern, St Elizabeth, as was Munro, though after a student died of a burst appendix, Alice never went back. Mary comments dryly that their education really was chaotic. Tom would leave for the US four years later at the age of twenty-one to claim his citizenship, never to live in Jamaica again. He went to live with his late Aunt Helen's family, the Lawrences, but his life in the US would be a tragedy in many ways.

When Berenice was in hospital with typhoid fever, Courtville didn't yet have a telephone, so Mr Powell came across the street regularly with updates from the hospital about her condition. Mary remembers her father going to visit her mother every day and spending hours there. In the same breath, she reminded me defensively that he also had the responsibility of taking care of the children. Mary was taken to visit her mother in hospital once, and clearly remembers the optimistic expectations from adults that her mother was on the road to recovery and would soon be home. But the prescribed enemas, says Mary, is what killed her. "She should never have had that!"

As an aside, I want to share a letter from Tahiti Berenice, Mary's niece, on this subject. It was characterized by a charming if skittish tendency to evoke horoscope charts as an explanation for everything. But despite colourful superstition, it made me stop and think. She writes:

Cycles have a tendency to repeat. As you found, Berenice died of a colon/ rectal haemorrhage. When Mary was young she had stomach problems and had to give herself enemas...how long for I don't know, but for several years I too had stomach problems due to being afraid to go to the loo in Africa...Was cured when I was in Switzerland, but I had a hemorrhoid operation when I was 27 or 28. Three-generation cycle.

Though I'm not even sure I understand her suggestion, I am not about to dismiss it. It may well point to a family weakness that might explain why a simple enema would have set off a haemorrhage in my grandmother resulting in her death. Whatever the explanation for the haemorrhage, she died far too young. Mary remembers her mother's body being brought back to Courtville, which she found awful, and her father constantly in tears. The Machados were always there for support. The funeral was held at St Andrew Parish Church, just across the road from the house. Mary attended the funeral, which was a large one, but not the burial. Soon after the funeral she visited the cemetery with her father when he went to put roses on her mother's grave.

Despite the recent plans for the family to emigrate, Major decided to remain in Jamaica and raise the family, a decision I can't fault because had they emigrated, my father would never have met my mother and there would be no me to tell this tale.

12

Thomas Briggs's Will and Trust

Consider the Major's life now. He has lost his wife, the mother of their five children. He had three more children with Josephine. Whereas Harold used to have Berenice to care for the kids, and plenty of time to sire another family in the long breaks when she was away visiting her parents, he was now responsible for his children's daily welfare. He had been a gentleman farmer, a cock fight enthusiast, a gun club member, volunteer soldier. His was a hedonistic existence, which had been funded by his wife's immense wealth. This is where Thomas Briggs's will and the trust fund comes in. It was a game-changer.

To understand what would become of Helen and Berenice's children after their mothers' deaths, one must follow the money, as they say; in other words, one must follow the wishes for Bostitch and its future owners as expressed in Thomas Briggs's will. Thomas Briggs was shrewd and meticulous. His planning was always methodical and his last will dated October 30, 1917, is proof of that. I have a copy of the will that was sent to me by the Rhode Island Hospital Trust around 1977 when I was tidying up loose ends for my dad, who had left Jamaica a few years before. After my work was done I put it in my files and never laid eyes on it again until I began doing research for this book. The copy had turned quite dark and Carole and I carefully retyped it to allow for easy reading and quick reference. Here was I, a Jamaican great-grandchild of Thomas Briggs, reading a will that he had executed one hundred years before, and trying to understand his thought process as he protected and provided for the grandchildren and great-grandchildren yet unborn.

With his eldest daughter Helen dead at twenty-seven in 1906, and his younger daughter Berenice running off to Jamaica in 1912 with a charming rogue, Briggs made the smart decision to protect his grandchildren by creating two trusts with equal amounts for each child: one for Helen's children and the other for Berenice's. The trusts remained in effect for twenty-one years after his death, and it had the effect of keeping these seven motherless kids together as owners of 90 per cent of Bostitch shares. No one could sell their holdings. For Harold, the fact that he would not be able to get his hands on Berenice's inheritance must have come as a shock.

Briggs would have been painfully aware that while Helen had married a hard-working young man, Dana Lawrence, who proved to be an asset to Bostitch, Berenice's choice was a flamboyant opportunist. But Briggs also would have realized that only Helen's youngest son, Leonard, an MIT-graduated engineer, had taken a keen interest in the business at a young age and had the skill-set to add value to the business. Robert, Helen's eldest son, was a veterinarian and farmer and never got along with Leonard while Marian, the eldest child, probably had no interest; women in America never even had a vote until 1920, let alone were involved in the corporate world.

On the Melville side the grandchildren were much younger. Briggs knew Major well, and it wouldn't have taken him long to figure out he was not businesslike. Besides, the Melvilles lived in the Caribbean, not in Rhode Island. By establishing the trust, Briggs ensured that should anything happen to Berenice, only her children and not her husband, would benefit from his life's work. They would receive their dividends but would not be able to dispose of their shares until the trust came to an end, twenty-one years after his death.

When Briggs died on September 24, 1928, he owned 90 per cent of Bostitch, as well as other stocks, bonds, and real estate, including his house at 60 South Angell Street in Providence and a winter home in Altamonte Springs, Florida, now a suburb north of Orlando. On his death, the shareholding of Bostitch was as follows: Thomas's 90 per cent was divided equally between the three Lawrence kids and the five Melville kids. The other 10 per cent of the company was owned by two of his key employees from the very early days: 5 per cent by Joe Whalen, by then the president of the corporation, and 5 per cent by a Mr Maynard, then a vice-president of Bostitch.

The first few clauses of Thomas Briggs's will dealt with his personal effects and provided for his second wife Esther Knight, his sister Lydia Seekell, and his cousin Susan Davis with income for the rest of their lives. The vast majority of the estate was left to the Rhode Island Hospital Trust to be held in trust. Briggs had a vision for Bostitch, the company he founded and built from scratch, and his will allowed his trustees to manage the other assets in the estate in the way they saw fit, but they were instructed in no uncertain terms to 'preserve the investment' in Bostitch.

As it turned out, of course, my grandmother died in 1930, only two years after her father's death. The Melville children were now joined at the hip financially with the Lawrence children as Bostitch's motherless owners. And when in 1942 my uncle Douglas was killed in the Second World War, since he had no children his share of the dividends was split among his four siblings under the terms of the will, bringing the total number of beneficiaries down to seven: three Lawrences and four Melvilles.

Harold would soon discover that no money had been left for him, and the only access he had to Berenice's vast wealth was as the guardian of their children. He would have to regularly apply to the trustees in Rhode Island for amounts they would have to approve.

The children had become the key to unlocking any funds the Major would now want or need. Therefore, he'd spare no expense on their behalf. After all, this was his only way to tap into the proceeds of the trust.

13

The Ivy Parks Years

*I*t had to be difficult for Harold as a widower coping with five children, so it's not surprising that he'd soon feel the drum roll of change. He made a five-week trip to the US in October 1931, almost a year after Berenice's death, probably to settle affairs regarding the American property Berenice had bought before her death, and almost certainly to visit the trustees. Then, soon after his return to Jamaica, an American 'housekeeper' he had met on his trip arrived, a Miss Isabel Raab whom the Major had hired to oversee the staff and assist with the children. It would've been easy for the Major to justify to the trustees the expense of a governess; the children would require a woman's touch to assist with their upbringing. Miss Raab would become a daily presence in the home.

I don't know the date she first arrived in Jamaica, but the Daily Gleaner describes Isabel and the Major at a dinner dance on January 19, 1932, at the reopening of the Constant Spring Hotel, where, it was stated, "...a brilliant assembly of people from all over the island enjoyed themselves in gorgeous tropical setting." On July 7, the newspaper's caption under a picture of Isabel states, "Here On

Second Visit: Miss Isabel Raab of New York was among the prominent passengers who arrived here yesterday in the liner Quirigua. *This is Miss Raab's second visit to Jamaica since the first of the year.*" A third mention comes in a *Gleaner* caption under a picture of the pair on October 1: "*Trying To Spot A Winner: Major Melville and Miss Raab snapped at the Marlie races on Wednesday.*" This is a reference to the Marlie racecourse in Old Harbour, St Catherine affectionately known as Little Ascot.

It would appear from that photo caption that she was much more than a governess or a maid. Mary remembers her although, as always protective of her father, she dismissed Miss Raab when I brought up the subject. At the mention of her name, Mary sat straight up in her chair with a jerk: "Oh her! She was just the maid!" Never mind that it was unlikely there were any white maids in Jamaica then, or now.

But Isabel Raab appeared to have been a 'friend with benefits' and from her travel records, she made three lengthy trips to Jamaica, the first late in 1931, and two more during 1932. But she was to be a passing fancy, and she returned to the US in December that year, as soon as a certain Mrs Ivy Parks came on the scene.

After the booting of Miss Raab, the situation in Harold's domestic life would give rise to much gossip and speculation that survives to this day. There is no doubt that the depth of the relationship between the Parks and Melville families that went on for at least five years would, for better or worse, run deep. It included frequent deception, many trips, lavish spending and real estate purchases that no doubt contributed to Ivy becoming a very rich woman.

Harold had his sights set on Ivy Parks, a white Jamaican, to replace Miss Raab as 'caregiver'. He soon hired her as the governess for his five children and, not surprisingly, ended up having an ongoing affair with her. This was especially scandalous as she was married to Basil Parks, a prominent businessman from a white Jamaican family. They had three kids, the eldest of whom was none other than Lucille Iremonger who wrote the chapter about Major in her book *Yes, My Darling Daughter,* which had been delivered to me years later at Chukka Cove by her little brother, Ivy's youngest child, Wally Parks. The Major and Mrs Parks seemed to have had much in common. They were both fun-loving and loved to travel; while Basil Parks was sixteen years older than his wife, Major and Ivy were a bit closer in age, Major eleven years older than Ivy.

It doesn't seem as though Mrs Parks behaved like a governess should, simply teaching and providing guidance to the Melville children. Instead, she gallivanted around with the Major, taking local and even foreign trips with him as he lavished her and her children with presents. The three elder Melville kids were already teenagers, and would have been old enough to know, or at least sense, what was going on. But what was strange was that Ivy's husband seemed to take more interest in Harold's children's education than in what his wife was up to, making it easy for Harold to worm his way into the Parks family.

Lucille Parks had a younger sister, Phyllis, of whom Mary said "she was the nicest one." In addition, there was "this nasty, spoiled little boy who was about four years old then." This of course would have been Wally.

When I said, "So that's why Major took him under his wing?" her answer was, eyebrows raised, "He tried but it was a waste of time." Mary's sister Alice who later went to New Zealand to visit her son who was living there, reported back to Mary that Wally was telling anyone in New Zealand who'd listen that the Major was his father! Mary told us she dined with Lucille and her husband once when visiting London, and in return Lucille and her husband overnighted in Scotland with her and her husband, Dr

Innis Lumsden. Mary said Lucille was a dreadful social climber and snob, and her father Basil was a nasty man. She also told me that Lucille ended up going to Oxford University, and said, "I cannot remember what degree she did, but I never liked her!" When you consider that both families were being affected by interlopers, it's quite likely Lucille felt the same way about Mary.

I always found it strange that this very unorthodox relationship between Mrs Parks and Harold could take place in plain view, resulting in a strained triangle; Mary shared a memory that offered a possible explanation. Basil's business partner was Mr Walter Durie, an Englishman who had established a very successful business in the island and who lived in the great house in Cherry Gardens in Kingston. Mary says Mr Durie died quite young and it appears his widow became Basil's mistress. She remembers Basil taking herself and young Walter up to the house where the guides or brownies were having some event with activities in the garden and they were told to go out and play with them out of the house. Basil disappeared inside with Mrs Durie for the afternoon which struck Mary as pretty odd. This would explain why Basil was quite sanguine about the affair going on under his nose. I cannot help wondering, given Wally's obvious loyalty, affection, and fascination with the Major and his eagerness to identify as his son whether, in fact, he was his son. Maybe the affair went on for longer than realized.

In her book, Lucille Iremonger brings this time to life, corroborating what we think we know, and filling in gaps in the story. I mentioned earlier that Lucille writes of being taken by her mother to meet the Major and his family at their home. She was disappointed by the large but rather shabby Courtville, its lawns dried out and cracked; obviously Major's horses had chewed the property grassless and trodden it down. The home had been bought to accommodate the large family. Something Lucille wrote about the visit made me sad: "I do not now remember at exactly what moment it was that I realized we were on show, my sister and I, in our new dresses, as loved, cosseted, well-looked-after children, incomparably more blessed than, and leading a very different existence from, these motherless waifs."

Lucille describes them all going to what seemed to be depressing old Courtville for one of the Major's feasts with 'curry goat and rice and peas', or black crabs or Blue Point oysters in season, which Mrs Parks shared 'a taste for'. But it was mostly the Melvilles who would turn up at their house, not the other way around. In short order, the Major began arriving for morning coffee, bringing some or all of what she described as the Major's 'orphans', and sometimes staying all day. When Major didn't take off with their mother, he often invited the Parks girls to join them for a movie. The house would be filled with this family until well into the night; Basil Parks, so much older than his wife and clearly a bit of a bore, took off to bed by 11:00 p.m., uninterested in movies or social chit chat. Lucille describes their usually quiet household as then becoming 'a social maelstrom'.

Lucille's mother became a hedonistic party animal, going with Major to the movies, or he'd come to pick up Ivy and she'd leave with him for the entire day, supposedly looking at properties for investment, and return sunburnt and happy. They too attended social events publicly: the *Daily Gleaner* featured them at a concert raising funds for an anti-T.B. drive; at the inaugural ceremony of Kingston Voters Civic, which Basil Parks presided over; and at art exhibitions and even a cricket match.

But Basil Parks played an intriguing role in all of this, too. While his wife came under the spell of the charismatic Major and the distraction of this 'new, seething social life', instead of putting an end to it, he enthusiastically offered guidance to the Melville kids as he thought they should all be educated in England. I wonder how Lucille felt when her own father, who'd always tended his children's education with fixity of purpose, now embraced, as his new project, these "orphan kids" he considered poorly educated. Why? Because Basil Parks felt stuck in Jamaica. His English family had migrated to Jamaica before Basil was born, and his ambition had been to restore his own children's heritage "of which he had been deprived by his father's hapless decision to emigrate", according to Lucille. He wanted his children to have educational keys to the seat of the British Empire.

That Mr Parks found my father and his siblings' education to have been sorely neglected is telling. These motherless 'trust fund babies' seemed to have lived wildly, without routine or formal education. And there was this hapless older man holding onto the shape of his home, feverishly ensuring a way out for his children and those of Major, maybe trying to gain some control of an untenable situation by taking on these extra five children's education as his project. He probably hoped their father would follow them to England.

Having tutored his own bright daughter, Lucille, and hiring special coaches for her and also ensuring Phyllis and Wally were well educated, Parks was horrified at how little the Melville children knew. It was obvious my dad, by then in his mid-teens, was not cut out to be a scholar; he only wanted to ride horses and shoot birds, and like me he was probably dyslexic. This didn't seem to faze Basil, though Douglas was the only Melville son who would end up at university. As for the girls, in those days, most became secretaries, nurses or housewives, but this didn't dampen Basil's enthusiasm either. He made sure they too had a chance at education; in fact, his own daughter Lucille would go to Oxford, where she'd meet and marry her husband, Thomas Iremonger. They ended up moving to the South Pacific during the war; her husband would later become a noted Tory politician in England.

In this strange triangular relationship engendered by his wife, Basil became engrossed with the fate of the Melville children and had a great influence on the eventual direction of their schooling. His own children he'd already scolded, cajoled, and encouraged, inspired and exhausted with work. Now he had found these waifs whose future he felt empowered to shape with access through Harold into the deep pocket of their trust. And the Major was happy to relinquish the responsibility and be rid of the task; after all, the children's trust fund would pay for whatever Mr Parks designed for them. Basil had prospectuses, brochures, and contacts for the best schools, acquired while planning for his own children's future, and it was easy for him to pinpoint institutions where Major's children should be educated.

Tom, the eldest, was seventeen when his mother died in 1930 and was never sent to school in England. His earlier schooling was in Kingston, but he was later sent to Munro College. For whatever reason, the Melville children were moved around a lot for their education. Douglas also attended Munro College for a while; his name appears on a plaque there listing former students who lost their lives in the Second World War. At Munro, Tom apparently got into several fights. In my mind he was the rebel in the family; he was also an American by birth, and all he wanted to do was get to hell away from the Major, Miss Raab, Mrs Parks, and the chaos of living at Courtville, where the extended family included Major's cousin Owen Silvera and his family. He just wanted to return to the land of his and his mother's birth, which he did the day he turned twenty-one in 1934; he would visit Jamaica twice in 1935 and again in 1939, leaving in January 1940 never to return.

Perhaps Basil Parks would have been more hesitant to assume this role in the Melville children's lives had he realized that having established the need for them to go to school in England, the Major would plan the journey to take Alice, and insist he be accompanied by Basil's wife. Mrs Parks also insisted that her husband allow her to go because Alice needed a suitable chaperone. This threatened to set off a firestorm of gossip in Jamaica and even the long-suffering Basil tried to put his foot down. Harold Melville and his family taking over his wife and his home was apparently acceptable, but travelling together to England, even with the children, was surely beyond the pale. But Ivy stood her ground, insisting the Major could not manage alone; after all, it was her husband's dream they were fulfilling.

She not only got her way but secured a signed affidavit from her husband stating that she went with the Major to ensure the well-being of his poor motherless children with his full consent and blessing. Soon the pair was off to England to settle Alice at Wychwood, a boarding school in Oxford. They left at the end of September 1933, not returning to Jamaica until January 1934 – an entire school term. The trip was a great success, Alice was settled into her school, and Mrs Parks returned with many gifts from the Major, including jodhpurs from Saville Row and a 12-bore shotgun. Five months later Basil himself took Lucille, 18, Wally, 6, my dad, 18, and my uncle Douglas, 15, to England, arriving May 7, 1934, leaving his wife with Major for two months. Basil returned to Jamaica with young Wally in July. By this time Mary was eleven and at boarding school at Hampton.

Ivy sailed to England again in June 1937 to accompany Mary, 13, to a convent school in North London – "Basil's idea!" says Mary – where in her first year she became very ill with measles and pneumonia. "The doctor said that I could not live another winter," she told me. "I had to be sent back to Jamaica." I imagine she was overjoyed to return to her home and her father. In a curious footnote, she would return to Jamaica on the same ship with my dad and mum from their honeymoon in July 1937. Ivy inveigled many free trips to England before it would fall apart as Major later got sick and broke; Ivy collected the last £600 from him and seems then to have bolted, probably laughing all the way to the bank!

It was a mysterious arrangement that made a cuckold of Basil. Reading the early chapters of Lucille's book gave me new insights into the arrangement. Both Basil and Ivy were orphaned at a young age; Ivy's family had been extremely wealthy but lost everything in the great Kingston earthquake and subsequent fire of 1907. It's possible Ivy married the older Basil seeking security, but lived a boring and unhappy life. The exciting Major came along and offered not just fun, travel, and gifts but as it turned out introduced her to land deals that made her independently rich. One senses from Lucille that Ivy was an opportunistic and somewhat greedy woman who always put herself first, even above her children. Interestingly, Lucille writes "my father was straight, honest, naïve, simple, stubborn and made for the slaughter. My mother was a bandit."

Reading Lucille's account of Major and Ivy's earlier trip, I was struck by her often made observation that the Major, no matter his eccentricities and inappropriate and often bullish behaviour, was a most affectionate and loving father. Had the children stayed in Jamaica with him, would their lives have been filled with a comforting family environment that they'd be deprived of faraway over the Atlantic at boarding school? I also remembered Wally's obvious affection for the Major, who taught him how to shoot, perhaps filling the role model of sportsman figure in the life of a little boy whose serious, indoor, much older father was only obsessed with education. The Major and Wally had bonded; Wally wanted me to be aware that Major was someone he cared about, someone he didn't find eccentric, but rather a flamboyant 'man's man', a charmer of women. He was clearly a hero to one little boy.

For the teenaged Lucille, the affair obviously affected her negatively. How did it affect the Melville children? I didn't detect the same animosity from Mary towards Mrs Parks as there was towards Miss Raab. She had nothing but contempt for the American governess. Alice did not like Miss Raab either, but they both felt differently about Mrs Parks. Maybe it was because they met Ivy within a family situation; Basil was a family friend. They might also have realized that Ivy was more central to their father's life.

My Uncle Tom and Lucille Parks, close in age, became great friends and were considered 'going together'. There is a lovely black and white picture that Wally sent me of Tom and Lucille sprawled contentedly beside each other in sunshine on the lawn like any young couple that could easily be assumed to be teenage romance. It definitely reflects a close bond. But that going together may have reflected their fervent conspiratorial wish to get out of this madness, a virtual family circus, and leave Jamaica.

In a photograph of the Major and Ivy that Wally also sent me after his visit to Chukka Cove in 1993, the Major is suavely dressed in a dark single-breast sports jacket buttoned casually once over his massive chest, white slacks, and white leather shoes that were fashionable in the day. Standing tall, sturdy, and striking, his extra pounds easily absorbed by his height, dark hair slicked back to one side, he exudes command and confidence. Sweetly smiling at his side, almost a foot shorter, leaning towards him fondly and trustingly, is the pleasant figure of Ivy, in a gently flowing white summer dress modestly below the knee, and belted at the waist; she's wearing low white pumps with an ankle strap. Her bare arms reveal the unmuscular softness expected of gentlewomen of the day. The picture as they say paints a thousand words: the dashing figure of Major that Lucille describes, proudly posing with her mother at his side, his latest doting conquest. One wonders who took the picture.

I have no doubt that Jamaica, with its taste for small island gossip, knew that Mr Parks was being humiliated. At one point, Ivy Parks and Major may have been living together or at the least she was sleeping over a lot. This came out in an embarrassing way when Major's house was robbed and personal stuff belonging to *both* of them was stolen from the bedroom; and all of this reported in great detail in the local papers. Perhaps the only thing Basil Parks had control over was his own home, so he stayed put while his wife was out gallivanting. The robber would get a five-year prison sentence.

I suspect everyone in the social circles of Jamaica at the time would have realized that Mrs Parks fulfilled roles in Major's family other than that of a governess. Besides their infamous voyage to England, she was at his side at most social events in Kingston. Yet for all the hurt Lucille felt for her cuckolded and humiliated father, which is painfully obvious in her book as she told the story some thirty years later, Lucille describes the Major as an affectionate, warm man who indulged all five of his children with displays of tenderness. Not so her self-centred and distant mother who scarcely touched her own three children. Lucille wonders if her mother on reflection had been troubled by the fact that unlike Harold, she found it so difficult to be warm. Because, in an amusing and telling story Lucille shares about an incident after her mother's return from the trip, she describes her mother inviting her to sit on her lap. When Lucille obeys, a period of silent discomfort follows, shortly after which her mother abandons it as a failed experiment, never to try it again.

If on his extended trip to England Major had discovered that, rather than a nurturing proxy mother for his children he had on his hands a cold-hearted schemer, it didn't end the relationship. There is a very telling scene in Lucille's book that's indicative of the Major and Ivy years: Thanks to her father Basil's search for the best tutors, Lucille won a scholarship to England. On the day she received the news of her success she was in school and was given the rest of the day off. Leaving through the school's grand entrance hall, she was faced with the improbable sight of the giant Major and her diminutive mother waiting to celebrate the news with her.

Lucille describes the pair arriving at her school that day when she was let out early thanks to winning the scholarship. They came to take her to lunch at the fashionable Myrtle Bank Hotel, the height of Kingston society they frequented. It highlights something that must have troubled Lucille: the uncomfortable absence of her father, Basil Parks. For it was Lucille who knew how richly he, and he alone, deserved the joy of this victory.

14

The Unravelling of The Major

Owen Silvera is Major's cousin from his mother's side, and his presence as live-in horse trainer at Courtville not long after Berenice's death signalled a new energy in the Major's self-indulgent life. If cockfighting, skeet shooting, and racehorses had been hobbies before, his racehorse fascination became much more than that. There are many newspaper reports between June and July 1932 of Major's new and clearly extravagant acquisitions, including news of *Toy*, an imported bay filly of *Achtoi* lineage. *Toy* was the offspring of a Gold Cup winner, *Santoi*; in fact, *Achtoi's* progeny were all major race winners and purse money earners. By August an agricultural show at Knutsford Park features horses bought from the Major, handled by Owen Silvera whom the report notes 'is becoming recognised as one of the best trainers in the country'. My dad even gets a mention in one of the show events, called tilting. The paper reports that a 16-year-old 'Johnny Melville caused a burst of applause by tipping the first ring and taking the second clear in succession.'.

I wonder what it was like for the five children, their mother gone, to see their father spending their inheritance on women and horses. Mary recalls that the Silveras' presence in their lives was a negative influence on her father. Owen encouraged an already eager Major in his extravagant spending on horses. In September 1932 Major upped the ante. He acquired another racehorse, an American-bred mare, *Mary Nardo*, said to be fast as lightning, and also retained his own jockey. Though Owen Silvera, who was fondly referred to as Owen 'Banker' Silvera, became a catalyst in Major's eventual financial ruin, my father John remained close with him. I remember when I was a child that every Tuesday, Dad and Mum went to Kingston for business and shopping, and always paid a visit to Owen's stables on Molynes Road.

Basil Parks's investment of time in the Melville children left the Major with time on his hands for his various ventures and shenanigans. Meanwhile, Major continued his litigious ways with numerous cases either as plaintiff or defendant. He was the defendant in a paternity suit brought against him by a Miss Adlin Heron which went on for a few years. Major lost in court, appealed and eventually got a retrial, all pretty embarrassing for the children, one can imagine. It speaks volumes about his character. Major's lawyer argued in what appears to be at least two trials, the second at appeal court, that the child could not be his. No costs were awarded, which suggests that Adlin Heron couldn't prove he was the father. But I have no doubt that, given his record, he probably was!

As far as finding a steady way of making a living, Harold Melville, jack of all trades, master of all for a while, had no staying power. He tried business but he had no talent for that. He had tried everything – farming, beef and dairy cattle, even goats – and then he tried bananas. Although short-lived, his banana business thrived at the beginning, according to a *Gleaner* report in December 1931:

Possibilities of Banana growing in Lower St. Andrew. Deep well irrigation has results in magnificent cultivation on Beverley Farm and Pembroke Hall properties. Fruit grade at 90%. The question of the feasibility or otherwise of growing bananas in lower St. Andrew has been demonstrated once and for all by the result of deep well irrigation carried out recently on Major Melville's properties Beverley Farm and Pembroke Hall just below Halfway Tree. An Antonsanti well has been sunk on each of the properties and pumps installed giving a steady and apparently inexhaustible supply of water... The site of the two wells was determined first of all by the divining rod....

Major had the gift of water divining, one that Mary claimed to have also. This would have assisted in locating the underground water that would irrigate the banana properties.

And this: *"Only Four months old: A magnificent piece of banana cultivation on Pembroke Hall Estate. The plants are only four months growth, and are already approximately six feet in height."* An accompanying picture features Major Melville and Owen Silvera.

By 1932 Owen Silvera was bringing the Major much attention as a horse owner though I'm not sure what Silvera's connections were to the banana crops. Major became a director of Jamaica Banana Producers, was seen at the Ward Theatre where the governor was urging civic pride and clean administration. When in April 1934 young John and my uncle Douglas went to England to go to college, "where they will be prepared for university," it was Basil Parks and not the distracted Major who took them there.

By July 1935, Major is seen cavorting with Ivy Parks at a rum punch party at the Myrtle Bank Hotel hosted by the Jamaica Tourist Trade Development Board for the visiting members of the Pan American Medical Association. Despite the name of the

Board being a mouthful, it shows Jamaica's early commitment to the development of a tourist industry. Now considered a big-wig amongst the agricultural elite of Jamaica, Major is a specially invited guest at the November function of the Jamaica Agricultural Society's annual social at Liguanea Club. In 1936 Major is seen at Knutsford Park at various race meets wearing his white helmet, there again at a polo gymkhana where the small crowd was 'certainly representative of the best Society and the turf generally'. There are many mentions of Major at skeet shooting events; in one in 1937 he fails to place, and at the second he snatched the largest pool of the day at fourteen pounds.

Speaking of shooting, I'm reminded of one of my dad's memories of Major. He once told me Major had a pair of custom-made, matching Purdey 12-gauge side-by-side double-barrel shotguns, no doubt purchased on the extended trip he took with Ivy Parks to the UK. When he went to 'bird bush' he took with him a couple of boys to find and retrieve the pigeons and doves he shot and a man to carry his ammunition and load his guns. He would fire two shots from one Purdey, hand it to the man, and take the loaded one; that way, he could shoot almost continuously if the flight of doves was good. Dad told me he would fire until both guns got so hot he'd have to wait for them to cool.

In January 1937 Harold was presented with an efficiency decoration by Governor Denham at Up Park Camp and sworn in as a Justice of the Peace the following month. Sandwiched between these two events is an announcement more notable for me – my parents' marriage on February 11. My father married Janet Mima Hastings, "Spinster, Gentlewoman, Twenty-Two years old".

The rest of 1937 sees Major participating in too many skeet-shooting events to mention, but as his health began to fail in 1938, Major's life seemed to spin out of control. Ivy Parks appeared to have disappeared from the scene, and he's back to the horses, watching polo gymkhanas and Knutsford Park's Easter Parade. But then he's sued for a pound by an employee in some confoundingly unnecessary domestic dispute with a butleress! And that same year, he's sued for an unpaid electricity bill.

Then towards the end of the year, Harold Melville takes a second wife on November 3 – Daisy Enid Annie Reid, a spinster, nurse and twenty-one years younger than he was. In December the *Gleaner* reports his presence at the races with his new bride. If this all seems very abrupt, it's because that's all the information I have of that time – though I do know it was Enid who nursed him back to health when he got ill, and I suspect that's how they met. I later discovered through Aunt Mary who attended the wedding that the only family members on Major's side in attendance were his brother George and his wife under some duress. Neither my father nor mother attended. This marriage would produce three more sons, Richard, Bob, and James, and a daughter, Joan that for me meant three more uncles and an aunt!

And yet another abrupt turn of events comes the following month. On December 16, the Trustee in Bankruptcy in Kingston authorized Harold Melville's property, furniture, and personal effects be put up for sale by public auction.

***

Harold Melville's imminent bankruptcy must have been an inconvenient truth for a long time. As I mentioned, a paragraph in Lucille's chapter casts doubt on the Major's handling of his business affairs. She describes him stuffing envelopes in a drawer and opening only the letters that gave him pleasure, probably ignoring several notices from the mortgagee of overdue payments. He was competing in clay pigeon shoots and attending the races while being sued by the electric company for his unpaid light bill – fiddling while Rome burned. He had been a spoiled man all his life, spoiled by women, from his aunt down through his wife, his outside woman, his girlfriends, and even his children. Obviously, insolvency meant nothing to him. He testified he had been 'sold out', but isn't that what mortgagees do when they don't get paid?

On December 10, 1938, the following notice appears in the *Daily Gleaner. FOR SALE COURTVILLE Halfway Tree-residence standing on 2 1/2 acres of land, AND MOLYNES Rd, St. Andrew – containing 176 acres properties of Harold A. Melville. APPLY immediately to Manton & Hart, 71 Barry St, Kingston.*

Major was being sold out by the mortgagee; he was in serious debt, as evidenced by the fact he had sold the Pembroke Hall property in 1936 to my father for £11,000. By his own admission in court, Major stated that Berenice had bought him the property in 1930 for £3,000 several months before she died. Then he had to raise a mortgage to pay the balance. The mortgage eventually grew to £4,500. He sold the property to my dad, John, five years later, in January 1936, for £11,000 – meaning he even made a profit of £6,500 off his son. He used that profit to pay off other debts, including £600 to Mrs Parks.

What am I missing here?

Uncle Tom turned twenty-one in August 1934 and took off to America to claim his US citizenship and his share of his mother's estate. By 1938 John and Alice were also of age to claim theirs, so when Major went bust only two children, Douglas and Mary, were under the legal age of twenty-one. Was Major finally coming to the realization that when Mary turned twenty-one in 1944, he would lose his grip on the funding that allowed him to live the lifestyle to which he had become accustomed since he had married Berenice in 1912? After his bankruptcy, he attempted to obtain money from his children's inheritance in Rhode Island to pay his debts. It was Leonard Lawrence, Helen's youngest son, who put a stop to that on behalf of his Jamaican cousins.

In February 1939, there is a summons for hearings on the Major's bankruptcy in The Supreme Court in Kingston. As we know, money had not been a problem while the children were minors, as Major was in control of their income. However, as each child turned twenty-one, they received their dividends directly from the trust. By 1939, the year of the Major's bankruptcy hearings, the fourth-born, Douglas, also came into his legacy, which left only Mary underage. That year, Douglas helped Major pay for another rural property in Jamaica, Mt. George in Yallahs, St Thomas.

Then disaster struck; Douglas was killed in the war in 1942, just five months before his twenty-fourth birthday. This triggered a series of events that eventually involved lawyers in Jamaica and lawyers for the trustees in Rhode Island. The story played out in the verandah gossip of Kingston's upper-class society, and in the court of public opinion. This led to a monumental rift in the Melville family that has never totally healed. As far as I'm concerned, it revealed the truest picture of my grandfather, Harold Melville, as a man who, though he cut a dashing and charming figure, and despite showing outward affection for his children when they were around, was at heart a cold and manipulative opportunist who seemed to have no moral underpinnings at all.

The Major's lavish and irresponsible spending spree since his wife's death – racehorses, prize cattle, overseas travel, Miss Raab, and of course Mrs Parks – was out of control. He seemed to have no conscience; having used his wife all those years, he used his children's trust funds to underwrite his way of life with its expansive enthusiasms, and would prove himself to be unscrupulous enough later on, when their money was out of his reach, to use their generosity shamelessly.

After Douglas died, his sisters, Alice and Mary, searched his flat in England but could not locate a will anywhere and there was no will to be found in Jamaica. Douglas had died intestate. Major applied for and was granted Letters of Administration by the Supreme Court of Jamaica on March 27, 1944, and through solicitors in the United Kingdom, for the Sealing of Letters of Administration on December 2, 1944. For the purpose of administration, Major listed Douglas's address as 'late of Mount George, Yallahs, St Thomas, Jamaica,' the property that Douglas had assisted his father to acquire. A notice appeared on March 23, 1945, in the England and Wales National Probate Calendar awarding "effects of £11,639 pounds and 1 shilling" to Major.

No one knows what was going through Major's mind. Did he really believe that having been granted administration for some cash Douglas had in a bank in England that he was entitled to all of his estate? Had he not read Thomas Briggs's will? Had he chosen to ignore it? The letters of administration entitled him only to the money and personal effects Douglas had in the UK, along with any personal effects he may have left behind in Jamaica. To quote from the relevant section of Briggs's 1917 will:

...one half shall be set off in trust for my daughter, BERENICE BRIGGS MELVILLE, the income thereof to be paid over to her for and during her natural life; and upon her death, if she shall die within twenty-one years after my death, the income from this one half to be paid over to her children, or the descendants of deceased children, per stirpes and not per capita, for twenty-one years after my death...

Berenice died within two years of her father.

The will goes on to state that at the end of twenty-one years:

*...this trust shall terminate and the corpus of this share of my estate shall
be paid over to her children or their descendants, per stirpes and not per
capita.*

The terms of the will could not have been clearer. The income
was to be paid to 'her children' or the 'descendants of deceased
children'. Douglas had no children so the trustees in Rhode Island
made the next quarterly dividend to the four surviving children of
Berenice, as directed by the will. There is nothing in the will that
allowed for any payment to be made to Major, or to any subsequent
kids he might have.

I have often wondered how the Major got away with all that
he did. Somehow all of Berenice's children but Mary shrunk away
from their father or any confrontation with him and sadly as a
consequence from the memory of Berenice, whose legacy would
make them self-sufficient; she became as unspoken as a family
secret. And all but my Dad left Jamaica.

There is a series of family photos taken before Berenice died.
The children were dressed and posed for it. There are photos of the
kids alone, kids with Major, Tom with Major, Tom with my dad,
every combination, but not a single photo that included Berenice.
I couldn't help wondering what had happened to pictures with
Berenice. We know Major was a bully, and overpowering, but
why would he allow the memory of his children's mother to die?
Was he that selfish and self-centred? That uncaring?

So what kind of memories would her children have of their
mother? There's not a lot to go on. From what I've learned of Tom,
much of it from Lucille's chapter, he was a kind and sensitive
person who bolted from Jamaica as soon as he was able. He wanted
to get as far away as he could from the Major and the memories of
his mother's death. Mary, for her part, was not yet seven when her
mother died, and her memories of her would have been limited and

susceptible to the Major's interpretations. Douglas died as a young man. That leaves my dad and Alice, who were fifteen and thirteen respectively when Berenice died; I keep asking myself what kind of memories of their mother did they hold? They were adolescents and within a few years of her death became adults; did Major affect them enough to wipe out any visible memory about their mother to the point where all they had to remind them of her was one profile photograph wearing a hat so you can't see her face, and a tiny, one-inch square cameo?

A small story has stuck in my mind as somehow relevant to my own father's silence about the past. It was about a toy, a red fire truck. The bitterness in the family was bad and it was petty. The story that Richard, eldest son of Major's second marriage, told me goes like this: around 1945, my dad gave him a red fire truck for Christmas. Richard remembers that Major made him return the gift. Now why, I wonder. That would have disappointed and puzzled a child to have to give up a present. How small a man to do a thing like that to a child?

***

My 96-year-old aunt Mary has an incredible memory. I interviewed her extensively for this book. She told me multiple times that Major told her he knew Briggs well, and he knew Briggs never intended any of the trust money to go to him. It appears he told his new family a different story, one that was about justifying his right to any inheritance from his late son, Douglas. Several decades later my uncle Richard told me that his father had told him that, 'Briggs's money was a curse'. It is true there was terrible tragedy in the family; it began with Helen's awful death in 1906 and continued with Berenice's death. But a curse? In life, sad though it is, people die. Did the money only become a curse when it ceased flowing through Berenice's hands or the children's trusts and into Major's?

In the mid-1940s when Major was challenging Thomas Briggs's will and trust, my dad, the complete opposite of his flamboyant father, bore the brunt of the stinging Jamaican gossip. How could the fabulously wealthy children of an American heiress not embrace their father, his new young bride, and their four half-siblings? A few years later my father moved us out of Kingston and into the 'bush' of St Ann. In hindsight I wonder if the reason he made the move was to get away from the gossip and bitterness in the city, because eventually it got really ugly. Lawyers from the trustees in Rhode Island arrived in Jamaica to advise Major's lawyers their only obligation was to the children of Berenice, not to him and his new family.

To end the feud, my aunt Mary, the baby of the family and the one most sympathetic to her father, proposed to her siblings a solution to the impasse. Although there was no legal reason to do so, the siblings agreed and instructed the trustees in Rhode Island that for ten years the dividends that would have accrued to Douglas be paid to Major, for his benefit and his new family. The contract had only one condition: if Major were to die within the ten years and should his wife remarry, the payments would cease. Major died in 1951 at age sixty-four of cardiac failure and diabetes, a few years after the agreement was implemented; his wife did not remarry until after the ten years had expired.

But the damage had been done and the bitterness continued for decades. Major's second family – or third, if you count the three sons he had with Josephine Silvera – were told, and would always believe, they'd been shafted out of 'their' inheritance. Years later my aunt Joan, the youngest child of Major and Enid, while visiting

Mary, her half-sister, in Scotland, railed about 'her' inheritance having been taken away by the children of the first marriage. Mary was astounded.

Major was never satisfied, always on the move, my grandmother Berenice had followed him around until she died, and then he kept on moving. He lived at Crescent in St Mary and Falmouth, Trelawny in the early years, then Belvedere, and Courtville, then at Mount George, St Thomas and Red Hills and Spring Garden in St Andrew. At some point, he bought Grange Pen in St Catherine. Obviously realizing he was dying he sold it only weeks before his death for over £20,000 to one of Jamaica's largest landowners, Henry George deLisser. At the time Grange was considered "one of the finest properties of its size in the parish" and to this day now subdivided into smaller stud farms it is where some of Jamaica's finest racing thoroughbreds are raised. The sale was obviously rushed as Major gave thirty-two head of the cattle on the property to his cousin Owen Silvera's son Laurie who paid for them after his death. Laurie Silvera would follow in his father's footsteps to become Jamaica's champion racehorse trainer, eventually moving to Canada where he was several times champion at Woodbine racetrack and a successful horse breeder.

Even what seemed like preparation made to have a presence in New England for the children to go to American universities was upended with Berenice's untimely death and Major went happily along with Basil Parks's educational initiative to send his children to school in England. The truth seems to be that Major was a rolling stone, and not even his children stalled him long enough to gather some moss on their behalf; their interests were never uppermost in his narcissistic mind.

***

I realized early on despite extensive research, that I knew very little about my grandfather. Now, as terrible as it sounds, I'm having a hard time coming up with anything nice to say about him.

But no one's perfect. And how many vivid characters are faultless? Major was charismatic. He devised a way to become 'the victim', and he played that card well even before he really deserved the title. He did become very ill in 1937, and all his bananas, which he'd started planting in 1931, had been blown down by storms. By Major's own testimony at his bankruptcy hearing:

He improved Molynes property by installing deep well pumps, planting 32 acres of bananas which were blown down many times and eventually destroyed by Black Spot Disease in 1937. He got sick and could not manage the property. In 1938 the property with bananas was ruined.

He was no businessman and he lived the high life on his wife's dime; when it caught up with him, he lashed out when he went bankrupt, blaming his children and conveniently forgetting about the fast women and slow racehorses in his stable. He blamed the weather, his illness, and everyone but himself for his bankrupt state.

I'm no angel and I've done many things in my life that I'm not proud of. But from all that I've learned, Major was a flamboyant, litigious, self-centred and irresponsible character who only looked out for himself. That's one way to see it. But then there's this: Had Harold and Berenice moved their family to the US in 1930 as planned, my father would not have met my mother, and I wouldn't be here to tell this story. Again, I do have to thank Major for my existence.

15

Aftermath: My Dad and His Siblings

The Major's tussling with his family over the will, in the aftermath of Douglas's death, was all happening during and immediately after the turbulent years of the Second World War. Each of my dad's siblings played a role in that war in one way or another except for my dad who was the only one still living in Jamaica back then, and as he was married with a young family he was not conscripted to fight for the mother country. And just as their mother's early demise would change her children's paths forever, so did the war.

Mary the youngest was the only child that remained behind in Jamaica when in 1934, assisted by Mr Parks, John and Douglas went away to England to school. Alice would follow a year later. My dad spent less than a year in the hands of a tutor before returning home; he was definitely not the academic type. Clearly, Alice was concerned about her little sister left alone back in Jamaica. In many ways she stepped into her mother's role. In 1937, travelling with Ivy Parks, Mary went to The Convent, Highgate Road, in London. As we know, she got very sick and returned to Jamaica in May 1938.

Alice was persistent; Mary should be sent to Wychwood boarding school in Oxford. Alice was not happy about Major remarrying and made a brief visit to Jamaica in December 1938, a month after he had tied the knot. Did Major even tell his eldest daughter beforehand he was getting married? Alice obviously laid down the law and in May 1939 Mary was on her way back to England with Douglas, who'd visited Jamaica for a holiday.

On September 1, 1939, the war broke out and Alice, Douglas, and Mary were trapped in England. By then, Thomas was living in the United States and would later enlist in the US army. Douglas joined the Royal Air Force Voluntary Reserve (RAFVR), and Mary got papers to go to one of the large hospitals in London, to train as a nurse. She was underage and needed her sister Alice's signature, but Alice refused so Mary decided to join the Women's Auxiliary Air Force (WAAF) and go into the nursing side. But before she could join up, Alice 'struck again', as Mary describes it. Her sister was now living on a farm owned by a family named Good. "She phoned me up and said, 'Do come and stay a week or two, I have landed up at this farm and the bedroom is huge and there is room in it for us both'", recalls Mary. "So I took two trains, one to London and then one to Aylesbury, where I was met by Alice. We had our meals with the Good family and during the chat at the table I told them what I was going to do. That was a mistake!"

Because there was a shortage of men for farm labour due to the war, a British civilian organization, the Woman's Land Army (WLA) was created. The women in this 'army' were referred to as Land Girls. They were placed on farms and paid by farmers to pick the crops and do what the men had done. Mr Good who'd lost many men to the army insisted that Mary would do far better as a Land Girl and that way, Douglas would have somewhere to stay any time he got leave from the air force; there would always be room for him. It was put in such a way that Mary felt that she would be selfish if she deprived Douglas of a place to spend his leave. Mary registered in the Land Army, as many did, and worked on the farm until the war was over.

Mary is strong willed, so I am convinced Alice had to trick her baby sister into becoming a Land Girl as London was a very dangerous place during the war what with all the bombing. Alice knew Mary would be much safer on a farm in the country. Mary returned to Jamaica for a holiday at the beginning of May 1945, just before the war ended mainly to be with her father whom she had not seen for five years.

The trip would prove fateful: "En route, of course, I met your dad," Mary writes to her daughter, Aussie Berenice. "The ship took six weeks to get to Jamaica, having called in to other West Indian islands before!" Time no doubt for her budding romance with the ship's doctor, Innis Lumsden, whom she would marry and settle with in the tiny village of Maybole, Ayrshire in Scotland. They would have two daughters, Berenice, named for her great-grandmother, and Anne. I remember Uncle Innis well; we saw a lot of him in my teenage years when they came every year to Jamaica. He had a great sense of humour and like any true Scot, loved his Scotch.

As for Alice, after leaving school she worked first as a private secretary at Eyre and Spottiswoode publishers, in London and attended the Royal College of Arts. She had a talent for painting, which according to Tahiti Berenice, she got from her mother. Alice met her future husband, Joseph Griffin, at a party in England during the war. He was born in Johannesburg, South Africa. Joseph's parents were English, and his father had gone to South

Africa to work as an engineer in the gold mines and bought a large citrus farm just outside Kruger National Park. Joseph had lied about his age in order to join the British army at seventeen and left on a troopship from Durban to sail to the UK. Probably a good horseman, he was then sent to Nigeria to train for the cavalry but got his knee kicked in and was sent back to the UK where he met and married Alice. Their children Joseph junior, Berenice, who I call Tahiti Berenice, and Jacky were born in England in a thatched cottage in Blewbury, Berkshire County. When the war ended, the family moved to South Africa and bought a citrus and cattle farm adjoining his parents' property, where Alice planted her garden and painted her landscapes. Alice's children were sent to boarding school in England, and sometimes went for two years without seeing their parents. In the holidays there were facilities like camps for the kids with horseback and bike riding, and swimming; Berenice remembers it as fun.

The three children returned to South Africa for two years of schooling in Johannesburg when their parents bought a flat there. But in 1956 the family moved to Switzerland because of political turmoil at home, the Mau Mau rebellion in Kenya, and unrest in Zimbabwe (Southern Rhodesia). Switzerland was their retreat and safe haven. Their safety net. But Geneva was a huge culture shock, and Joseph seems to have fallen off the rails. It must have been a mid-life crisis. He bought a Ferrari and a yacht, then another yacht. He was exuberant with his new surroundings. When he went down to Cannes to ready the boat for the family, a lady hustler nabbed him, "a master pro...she never left him for a second. Dad was a lamb thrown to the wolves..." commented his daughter Berenice. Alice gave him six months to make up his mind between them; they ended up divorcing. "It broke my mom's heart," says Berenice.

The loss of Douglas was a devastating blow to his siblings. Although he sailed to England in September 1937 to attend Cambridge University to study veterinary medicine, he could not have been there long for in 1939 he and his older sister Alice were living in a flat in the London Borough of Wandsworth. In what may have been a census or war registry he was listed as a 'student farmer', and Alice as a secretary. And then everything changed with the start of the Second World War.

Douglas would become a wireless operator and air gunner in the Royal Air Force Volunteer Reserve (RAFVR) and would achieve the rank of Sergeant. Of all the branches of the military for my uncle to serve King and Country, why did he have to choose the one with the highest death rate, the RAF Bomber Command? On June 20, 1942, my uncle Douglas was shot down over the Netherlands. It is believed his parachute didn't open. He was twenty-three. He is buried in the Ommen General Cemetery in that country.

My dad's big brother, Thomas Briggs Melville, namesake of his grandfather, Thomas Briggs, turned twenty-one in 1934 and a few days later sailed for the land of his birth. He was now an adult and would receive his share of his mother's estate directly from the trustees. For a while he stayed with his cousin Marian Lawrence Small, the eldest daughter of Berenice's sister, Helen. Marian's daughter, Helen, who was about thirteen at the time, remembers Tom living with them. It is worthy of note that although they lived in different countries, the children of Helen and Berenice Briggs looked out for each other, perhaps a tragic bond, given that their mothers had died so young. Not only did Tom go to live with his cousin Marian's family, but after the war when there was still rationing and shortages in England, Marian took a car and supplies to Mary in Scotland. They also attended their cousins' weddings across the Atlantic.

Tom travelled back to Jamaica twice in 1935 and around that time his cousin Leonard Lawrence arranged a job for him at the Boston Wire Stitcher Company. Even though Leonard was twelve years older than Tom, they had a good relationship. A 1936 Rhode Island State Census lists Tom as living in East Greenwich; occupation, clerk; industry, Wire Stitcher. So, there was a Melville that worked for Thomas Briggs's company for a few years, if only as a clerk. We will never know if he quit the job or was fired. Tom was back in Jamaica in 1939 for a couple months and then according to the US national census of 1940 he was living in South Kingston, Rhode Island, and listed as 'head of the household' with an elderly couple listed as 'boarders'. Tom was twenty-six years old and single, neither working nor seeking work. The form showed he had not worked for even one week or earned any wages in the previous year but that he received money from 'other' sources – the Briggs Trust Fund. Information from his draft card a year later shows Tom living in the picturesque Pawtuxet Village, which is at the confluence of the Pawtuxet and Providence Rivers, and again he is listed as unemployed.

The story told by my aunt Mary is that when visiting a good friend living in Cleveland they both got blind drunk one night, woke up the next day and enlisted in the army, making good on a dare. The army enlistment records confirm Tom, even though he was living in Rhode Island, did indeed enlist in Cleveland on April 3, 1941. Maybe he decided to enlist knowing he was about to be drafted anyway. Tom was a non-combat soldier with the rank of private. He worked as a laundry mechanic and later, when he was sent to England, an ambulance driver.

Tom contacted Mary when he arrived in England, and they arranged to meet in London, but she says he never showed up. They connected sometime later in 1942 just before the time that Douglas was killed. According to Mary, Tom was involved in an accident in a 'rehearsal invasion exercise' and shipped home to the US. I learned from the US war files that Tom was admitted to hospital in August 1944 and discharged in December in the 'line of duty'. His 'type of injury' was listed as a Disease, but the diagnosis was withheld by the National Archives and Records Administration (NARA). His disability was neuropsychiatric: Tom had gone crazy!

Declared a ward of the court, Tom went missing until 1948 when he was 'found' languishing in a veteran's hospital in Springfield, MA. Tom may have been an embarrassment to the family but how could he have been 'lost' for three or four years? Obviously, no one spent much time looking for him. I've never been able to get a rational explanation as to what really happened. Bear in mind that back in those days the accepted treatment for 'crazy' people was to keep them heavily sedated or restrained with the occasional electric shock therapy thrown in for good measure.

After Tom was 'found' in 1948, my father and Aunt Mary's husband, Dr Innis Lumsden, went to visit him. They found him very upset and hating where he was incarcerated; he had attempted to break out a couple times, which probably didn't make him popular with the staff. After a meeting with the head of the hospital, plans were put in motion to get him transferred to a private institution. Tom was eventually moved to the Chestnut Lodge in Rockville, Maryland. Around 1980 the Trust acknowledged Tom's siblings – he had no wife or children – as the legal heirs to his estate and, being aware he was in his late 60s and suffering from emphysema from a lifetime of smoking, with the court's approval they implemented basic estate planning.

Recognizing that Tom could never spend all his money in the time he had left on earth, and in an effort to reduce the amount of tax payable upon his death, the trustees proposed a gift $10,000 annually to each living sibling – John, Alice, and Mary – as well as to each of their children, eight, including me. These annual payments continued until Uncle Tom's death in April 1989.

After receiving my first $10,000 gift I wrote and thanked my uncle. To my pleasant surprise he sent a handwritten reply and we started a correspondence, which led to my flying from Jamaica to visit him at the Chestnut Lodge in Maryland in about 1981. Coming from Jamaica I had no idea what to expect and was not aware the Chestnut Lodge was a world-famous sanatorium. The Lodge, originally the Woodlawn Hotel, fell on hard times, and was purchased by Dr Ernest Luther Bullard from Milwaukee, Wisconsin, a surgeon and professor of psychiatry and neurology. Bullard renovated the building and reopened it in 1910 as a sanatorium for the care of nervous and mental diseases, renaming it Chestnut Lodge, nestled as it was among 125 chestnut trees on the grounds. For many years, Bullard was its sole physician, but over the next seventy-five years a total of three generations of the Bullard family operated the private hospital. Many nationally renowned therapists worked there over the years, and it was the site for a series of influential studies on the long-term treatment for psychiatric conditions. There was a two-year waiting list for patients to get in or for professors wanting to teach at this prestigious medical institution. It put Rockville on the map.

I first met with one of his doctors who brought me up to date with Tom's condition. I was happy to hear that he had improved enough that he was being weaned off his dependence on the only home he'd known for thirty years and now lived as an outpatient in a nearby house owned by the Lodge, with a live-in caregiver. He went to the Lodge daily for sessions with the therapists and had a driver who doubled as his valet.

The doctors had thought Tom delusional when he spoke about life growing up in Jamaica – his privileged island life, the surrounding elegance, the mahogany staircase and furniture at the family home in Kingston – they thought he'd created this in his mind, until I came to visit and confirmed that this indeed had been Tom's background. They appreciated my visit but wondered why his family had stayed away for so many years. Why had we abandoned him? I had no good answer, other than, from what I understood, Tom had been elusive.

Then I went to another building to meet this uncle whom I'd never before laid eyes on. Thomas looked an awful lot like my father although he had a full head of hair. He acted like he'd known me all my life and we talked about family and Jamaica. Suddenly, a stranger, a not-so-sane younger man, came pacing down the corridor to the end where we were sitting; he would stand for a minute and glare at me, never uttering a word, then turn and walk away, only to return in a few minutes to glare at me again. This went on for an hour or more. It was most unnerving, and I looked for the nearest window to plan my escape in the event the young man attacked. I was taking no chances as my dad had told me when he visited Tom decades earlier at the veterans' hospital, an inmate had taken a swing at him; he never went to see his brother again.

The following day I visited Uncle Tom at his home, and we went for a drive to look at some of the sights of Washington, DC. It was a few wonderful days and I thoroughly enjoyed my time with him. I would like to think my visit opened a door that helped to demystify 'crazy' Uncle Tom, because soon after that he was being visited by other family members and started going on trips with his caregiver to see family and take holidays as far away as Florida and even Scotland to visit his sister.

Sadly, on April 27, 1989, Uncle Tom died in Rockville. He was seventy-five. He is buried in the Swan Point Cemetery in Providence, where his famous grandfather, Thomas Briggs, and other family members are buried. It was a very small funeral: a couple of the trustees from the Rhode Island Hospital Trust, plus Tahiti Berenice and me from the family. After the funeral my cousin and I gave him a Jamaican send-off at an expensive restaurant with copious amounts of wine. Uncle Tom left his money to his siblings and nieces and nephews, including me, for which I am forever grateful.

Upon Tom's passing, there was one last hurdle: he had executed a will before he joined the army and his lawyer had written himself into that will as the sole beneficiary. It may not have been illegal to do that back in the 1930s, but it was totally unethical, particularly as the client suffered from schizophrenia. There was little chance the old will would have stood up in court, but the trustees chose to avoid a lengthy and expensive legal battle and made a settlement of $500,000, if memory serves me correctly, with the lawyer's son who had been assigned the interest by his shyster father who had died decades before Uncle Tom.

I treasure the brief and all-too-late relationship I had with my warm-hearted and generous uncle, and I regret not having known him sooner. He held no rancour toward his family and seemingly had no regrets about his life. But I can't help wondering about the way his life had fallen through the cracks: the loss of his mother; the apparent indifference of his father; the time he spent living with Helen's family and his relationship with Leonard when he relocated to the US; his job working in the 'family business'; the loss of his little brother Douglas; his own war experience and its aftermath. What had been the cost of that early neglect?

So, yet again, the untimely death of Berenice proved an insurmountable loss. But it comforted me to see Thomas buried at Swan Point in the same cemetery as his grandfather, at home in the end with his mother's family, safe in the bosom of their final burial place.

16

Dana and Leonard Lawrence

After the death of Thomas Briggs, the fate of the Bostitch Company came to rest heavily on the shoulders of his daughter Helen's husband, Dana Lawrence, and their youngest son, Leonard. There were three children in all, Marian the eldest and Robert the middle child. If Dana was a family man it wasn't so much in the sense of the all-American dad, but more in the role of a provider. No shirker, he went to work every day. His father-in-law, Thomas Briggs, valued his service to Bostitch whose operations he would improve over the years. Helen couldn't have dreamed how prophetic her words were to Anna, their teacher, about her children being left to her care, for soon, as we know, Dana would marry Anna, perhaps hoping to replace Helen both for himself and the children. She would bear him two more children, George and Lucy.

Many of the insights we glean about Dana are from a long letter Anna wrote, though we are not sure to whom, sometime after she and Dana married.

To Dana (as I knew him) responsibility was something to be assumed with fear and trembling. I have sometimes wondered if this was true of his childhood and younger days or whether it was a characteristic that developed during the days when he was suddenly left alone in strange surroundings with the responsibility of three small children. Whatever obligations he did assume he demanded perfection on his part even as he required it of others 'one hundred percent perfect is the way I want it.'

So, Dana was a perfectionist. He stayed at Bostitch for the next forty years (and in 1919, the *Rhode Island Pendulum* reported on the forgiveness of Dana's debts to Thomas Briggs out of kindness and recognition for his hard work at Bostitch). Again, from Anna's letter:

Dana had begun the task of making staples on an unpatented machine. A new machine, an imperfect machine – Dana who knew next to nothing about machinery – whose only mechanical experience had been guns, a motorboat and briefly...farm machinery. Dana who except for a few years had followed strict hours in his father's business in Quincy Market now began work at 7 a.m. until 6 p.m., with an hour at noon.

Dana also took on the compelling social issue of the day, Prohibition. In June 1918 he attended a huge meeting in East Greenwich's Town Hall in support of the Prohibition Amendment to the US constitution. This was an attempt to convince voters to support legislators who would ratify the 18th Amendment prohibiting the sale of alcohol, a priority for the 1918 election. Dana was unanimously elected to serve as the secretary of a local organization pushing for Prohibition to become law. Dana Lawrence was definitely nothing like the Melvilles.

It seems that, like their Melville cousins later, Dana and Helen's children's lives were far from straightforward after their mother died. This we know thanks in large part to a diary belonging to Alice Lawrence, Dana's sister who had gone to stay with her brother's motherless children for a time. I haven't seen this diary, but Helen's great-granddaughter, Marianne, shared some insights from it with me. Marianne wrote:

Dana Lawrence's sister came to care for the poor children in shock after the loss of their young mother. Alice was obviously overwhelmed and full of sympathy for the children. In her diary, Alice wrote that apparently Anna Lawrence, the stepmother, did much to drive Robert and Leonard apart so they wouldn't gang up on her. Anna had files on every family member to keep her stories straight. She was also a very smart lady, into genealogy and wrote a few local history books.

It was Dana's sister, Alice, and not the kids' grandmother, Helen's mother Alice Briggs, who came to their rescue. Maybe the new wife and stepmother wanted to distance the family from the Briggs side? Whatever the case, says Marianne, sharing what was in the diary, "My grandmother never spoke about her mother, and Robert once referred to her as 'the Briggs woman'."

Once they were old enough, none of Helen's kids stayed on with Dana and Anna. Marianne told me that her mother thought that after Alice Lawrence left, the children may have gone to other relatives. "I do know that Uncle George, Anna's son with Dana, lived with and was raised by Anna's parents, the Mathewsons, who were the caretakers at Goddard State Park. That's how he became interested in botany." Indeed, thanks to botany, George Lawrence was definitely the most successful of them all. He founded the Hunt Botanical Library at Carnegie Mellon University in Pittsburgh. In 1978 he was eulogized in an article that celebrated his contribution as an internationally recognized botanist.

Marianne goes on:

It is lovely and remarkable that of the three siblings, Robert [who went on to be a veterinarian and farmer in Holmdel, New Jersey] had the most enduring marriage, strongest faith, and was the most interested in family connections. He was especially solicitous of my mother [who would have been his niece] – taking her on trips, to the theater, etc.

Of Helen Briggs's eldest, Marian, she writes: *"I often think of the challenges my grandmother had to face at a young age and that she overcame them and did so much good in her life... I wish my grandmother had been more talkative,"* Marianne ends wistfully.

This feeling of the silence shrouding our family story had become familiar although there are a lot of silences in many families. Along with that comes a yearning we all seem to share for information to complete an unfinished tapestry, like the quest I find myself now pursuing, although I've left it a bit late. I suppose we never think to ask these questions when we are young because we are too busy getting on with our lives and we wait until those who know are either gone or too old to remember clearly.

In this sometimes frustrating quest there are many bright spots. At the time of her writing this, Marianne's 96-year-old mother, Helen, named for Helen Briggs, was in rehab after ten days in Cape Cod Hospital for COPD issues. "A long slog," Marianne explained to me. "I think meeting you was the highlight of the year for her." In my search, moments like those produced by this connection are both heart-warming and the source of even more questions.

I had never met cousin Marianne. We had been corresponding for several months, and she had provided me with useful information on the Lawrence side of the family. In June of 2019, Carole and I paid Marianne and her husband Bob Hirschman a visit in the seaside town of Brewster on Cape Cod. Bob and Marianne have a beautiful home in a wooded neighbourhood. They invited us out to dinner, collected us at our bed and breakfast where they greeted us most warmly making us feel truly like family. The following day we got a chance to look at the family trees and share photos at their home.

There is something special about meeting a long lost relative; it's like we'd known each other all our lives. This was a true manifestation of an invisible bond of DNA forged by Thomas Briggs so long ago. But the highlight of that visit was to meet Marianne's mother Helen Weishaar. Helen is the daughter of Marian Lawrence Small, who at ninety-six was warm and very funny and as sharp as my aunt Mary. We visited her first at her retirement home where we strolled the grounds and met her boyfriend also named Bob. In an energetic conversation we tried to bring each other up to date with a lifetime of family news. I was fascinated to discover that Helen remembered my uncle Tom, and that he lived with them for a while when he first arrived from Jamaica. This was another tiny tile of detail in the mosaic I was trying to build of my family history. We all went to a fancy dinner at a country club nearby, where Helen with Bob in tow in their easy companionship made the cutest couple, each having a martini before dinner. In a delightful coincidence the *maitre d'* was a charming Jamaican who worked there six months a year in the summer and now was delighted to find himself with Jamaican guests.

A couple months later we visited cousin Dorothy Lawrence in Sarasota, Florida. Dorothy is Robert Lawrence's daughter whom I'd met several times before but had not seen or been in touch with her for several decades. Dorothy is an incredibly young 91-year-old, slim, elegant and dressed to the nines. We had dinner at a private club by the sea in Old Sarasota, where Dorothy was greeted like family by the staff. She showed me her grandfather Dana Lawrence's pocket watch, handed down by her father Robert; inside was a photo of Dana's first wife Helen, daughter of Thomas Briggs. And here, seeing this tangible piece of memorabilia, I experienced once again an irreplaceable moment which placed me within reach of the Briggs legacy of which, however distantly, I had always been a part.

The youngest of Helen's children, Leonard, who was just five years old when his mother died, was also remarkable, and perhaps deserving of his own book. The only one of Helen's children to work at Bostitch alongside Dana, Leonard was a most handsome man with thoughtful eyes and an elegantly long face that suggested a guarded quietude. He was a complex man, Marianne shared with me, a genius. Her great-uncle was also very reclusive. "We never saw much of him; he never came to the beach house."

Despite his scientific mind, Leonard had an artistic soul. He played both the violin and the fife, and he was a regular patron of Boston Symphony concerts. He'd been deeply traumatized by the early loss of his mother, which may have accounted for his sensitive and reclusive nature. Marianne says he'd spend his after-school hours with his grandfather, Thomas Briggs, as a teenager, and later, as a mechanical engineering student at MIT, he worked in the holidays with his father, tinkering in the tool shop where he used his natural mechanical skills, helping out at Bostitch whenever needed. A short biography prepared by MIT on the dedication of a building there, funded by a bequest from Leonard, describes him thus:

> To some he was austere, taciturn and ascetic – a man difficult to engage in a conversation, impatient with trivialities, devoid of ostentation. To others he was warm, droll, and above all compassionate.

There are many instances of his thoughtful generosity, and his lifestyle reflected his impatience with ostentation. If his character was shaped at an early age by the disillusionment caused by the loss of his mother, the walls he built around himself kept safe a brilliant mind and a caring, cautious, unpretentious soul. As for his personal life, Marianne says he married once 'to a con artist whose first husband was in prison for embezzlement. After the divorce he had a long-time girlfriend'. As vice-president of Bostitch, Leonard loved the company his grandfather founded and enjoyed working there from 1930 shortly after his graduation from MIT.

Bostitch remained a private company with 90 per cent of its shares owned by Thomas Briggs up to his death. When Thomas Briggs made his 1917 will, Helen was already deceased. The moment Briggs died in 1928, the two trusts kicked in: one for the three Lawrence children, the other for Berenice. With Berenice's untimely death in 1930 the five Melville children became beneficiaries of that Trust. In 1949, twenty-one years after Thomas Briggs died, the trusts expired, and within a year or two there was a recommendation by the CEO Joe Whalen that Bostitch be sold to a public company in the same line of business. His argument was that this would give shareholders an exit strategy as they had been unable to dispose of their holdings for the life of the Trust. Leonard went to great lengths to block the proposed sale/merger, believing in this great company Thomas Briggs had built and which his father had served so faithfully. With great foresight he persuaded his sister Marian to join forces with him, but even together they could not block the sale as they controlled only 30 per cent of the Bostitch stock. Under Rhode Island law of the day, they would need to control more than 33.33 per cent in total; to merge a corporation needed a vote representing 66.66 per cent of its stock. So Leonard and Marian went to Scotland to negotiate with their cousin, my aunt Mary, but failed to gain her support to keep the company private.

Undeterred, Leonard offered his fellow vice-president and long-time associate, Mr Maynard, who owned 5 per cent of Bostitch's stock and was then seventy-five years old, $50,000 in exchange for an option to purchase his shares at nine-sevenths of book value and an irrevocable proxy to vote the stock. Maynard agreed to the deal which meant he got cash in hand; he continued to receive the dividends on his shares and was guaranteed a premium price when he sold or died. This proxy, along with Marian's support, put Leonard in control of 35 per cent of the Bostitch stock and enabled him to prevent the proposed merger. The combined ownership of all the other shareholders totalled 65 per cent, falling 1.66 per cent short of the amount required to allow the merger.

Leonard had outsmarted them all and succeeded in controlling the company, much to the dismay of the rest of the family and the CEO, Joe Whalen, who owned five per cent and was the architect of the proposed merger. Leonard had won hands down, and it probably gave him great pleasure, loner that he was, to have this control over his older brother Robert and his Melville cousins, most of whom really just wanted to sell the business, enjoy the proceeds and be free of each other. Having kept his distance from the family, Leonard would have been indifferent to their emotional response, deriving satisfaction from ensuring the wishes of Thomas Briggs as laid out in his will by safeguarding the status quo of Bostitch for many years to come.

As a scientist and the only family member working at his grandfather's great company, Leonard probably felt confident that he knew what was best for the company and his family, saving them from themselves and securing the value of the company for them all. He definitely did that. Some fifteen years later, Leonard, in his mid-60s and realizing he was terminally ill, orchestrated the sale of Bostitch to the conglomerate Textron in 1966. It seems he felt that if the company was going to be sold, he wanted it done on his terms, while he was still alive. He negotiated an excellent deal whereby the shareholders of Bostitch received 1.25 Textron shares for every one share they owned in Bostitch. Finally, after nearly forty years, the Lawrence and Melville cousins, the grandchildren of inventor Thomas Briggs, were no longer joined at the hip by their ownership of Bostitch. When Leonard died he left half of his estate to his *alma mater,* MIT, and the other half to his long-time girlfriend; he had no children.

I have no doubt that from his grave, Thomas Briggs must have been proud of Leonard's decision to protect his family and even more proud of him for completing his mission. Dana and his son certainly made their mark; through Dana and later Leonard's loyalty and diligence to Thomas Briggs and Bostitch, the Lawrence family would be blessed with their well-husbanded half of the massive Briggs fortune. And my great-aunt Helen would have been so proud of her youngest child's successes.

17

Crazy Gene

lbert Einstein said, *"The only difference between genius and insanity is that genius has its limits."*

Oscar Levant said, *"There's a fine line between genius and insanity. I have erased this line."*

You know where I'm going with this. Now that you've read this far about my family history, you've surely noticed that we are all fucking crazy. Psychologists have discovered that creative people have a gene in common which is also linked to psychosis and depression. Then there is the hand of fate, which is dealt to all of us. Sometimes we can't cope; don't want to have to cope. Each of us has our own sense of what is just and what is not. And there is nothing that sets off the voices of outrage within like perceived injustice. Perhaps 'going crazy' is a way to hush the impotence of those voices – the drowning of sorrows, the burying of frustrations. I've owned a simple black T-shirt with white lettering for at least the past twenty years; it's faded and tattered. I bought is as a joke, and Carole has tried to throw it out several times, and I've begged for it to be spared. Only since I started researching the family history and writing about 'The Crazy Genes' did it dawn on me why I'm so attached to the silly T-shirt: It reads, *You are just jealous because all the little voices are talking to me!*

But what is it about families? My friend Rachel points out to me that the first sentence of Tolstoy's novel *Anna Karenina* reads: '*Happy families are all alike; every unhappy family is unhappy in its own way*'. Whether we are forced to face and understand happiness or lack of it, or just content to bask in it, somewhere implicit in both ideas is that of family as the seat of the purest human emotion. Maybe that genius gene becomes the crazy gene depending on the health of that concept we call 'family'. So, where do I begin when it comes to mine?

On the face of it, for the genius gene, I only have to look at the story of my paternal great-grandfather, the inventor Thomas Briggs. I suppose my grandmother Berenice showed her crazy gene by marrying a stranger from Jamaica, dressed in a red dressing grown and told fortunes. But instinctively I seek elsewhere on the family tree for the insanity that I know nestles in me.

Besides Briggs blood, I also have Melville blood in me. And while doing family research it became obvious to me that Major was not normal. I also thought about H.P.C. Melville, Harold's father's cousin, who went from Jamaica as a young man to colonial British Guiana (present day Guyana) and 'married' two Amerindian women. Was he an adventurer or a little crazy? He fathered several half-caste children and created an ancestral line of European and Amerindian ranchers in the vast Rupununi region of Guyana, bordering the Brazilian Amazon. He eventually moved to England, where he was forever miserable sleeping in a bed, having got accustomed to a hammock. H.P.C. and Major's father being first cousins, I guarantee the stories of H.P.C.'s exploits would have found their way back to Jamaica and I could not help but draw a parallel between the two men. For sure, they both had our crazy gene.

Assembling the intricacies of genetics can be like fiddling with a Rubik's cube. We seek blocks of similar colour we know are related but getting them to line up is a challenge. I see similarities between H.P.C. and the Major, born almost a quarter of a century apart. First, there were the women. H.P.C. with his two Wapishana 'wives' and the Major with his concurrent families. British Guiana's Rupununi savannah and rural Jamaica can't really be compared, but they reflect rural sensibilities. Whereas H.P.C. in the tribal savannah could make up his social rules as he went along, the Major would have had to defy British colonial social mores and its expectations to accommodate his not so clandestine lifestyle. They both displayed hedonistic instincts in satisfying their lusts with little consideration for the women and children they may have hurt on the way. H.P.C. had no compunction about abandoning his Guyanese wives and ten children. Major showed a similarly cavalier attitude towards women: his legal wife, his common-law wife, and his many flings and way in which he used his children.

As I turn the cube around in my hands, I follow another colour, a different pattern forms. Later on, Major's mercurial business dealings remind me of another aspect of H.P.C. who imaginatively but often recklessly exploited the landscape around him. When rubber was in demand by the auto industry, the rubber trees of the Brazilian jungles became a commercial hub and H.P.C. was quick to see an opportunity to sell his vast holdings of cattle to Brazil. But when the rubber trees became diseased, the Brazilian rubber industry collapsed, and in 1910 the cattle industry of the Rupununi was severely set back. This was compounded by a British explorer,

Henry Wickham, who had smuggled thousands of seeds out of Brazil in 1876 that were then germinated at London's Kew Gardens. There were enough to jumpstart widespread cultivation in Malaysia. These Southeast Asia plantations were more efficient and out-produced those in Brazil.

The First World War had created a demand for cattle in Georgetown, the capital. H.P.C. persuaded the government to fund and develop a 'cattle trail' to transport live animals from the Rupununi to Georgetown. Construction began in 1917 and was completed two years later. The trail went from Lethem in the Rupununi to the Berbice River, where the cattle would go by steamer to the coast and then by rail to Georgetown. The trail from the savannah to Georgetown was a logistical nightmare, from wilderness territory through deep jungle, rainy seasons and swollen creeks, and fraught with setbacks not the least of which was the lack of any fencing. The first herd travelled the trail in 1920 with more than 70 per cent of the cattle vanishing into the deep forests probably into the welcome arms of grateful Amerindian dwellers there.

Before the trail was complete, H.P.C. sold out his interest to unwitting buyers; any bets he saw the writing on the wall? Though the cattle trail would prove to be a gigantic failure, the new owners persisted and it would be years before his purchasers realized their mistake and it was eventually closed for good in 1953. H.P.C. moved to England in 1923, married an English woman, Ethel, in 1924, and died in 1927. The U.K. probate of 1928 showed he left the princely sum of £249 5s 9d to Ethel. I wonder if he told Ethel about the ten children and two wives he'd forsaken back in South America? Major mirrored him not just with a roving eye but misguided forays into agriculture. Ironically, one such foray turned out to be that aborted plan to establish a rubber plantation in Malaysia in 1924. Some say there is no such thing as a coincidence. My wife would call it Karma.

As I learn more about my various strands of DNA, I realize we have issues on all sides: Briggs, Lawrence, and Melville. And by issues I mean that whether it's recklessness or just bucking the system, we all had in common a certain non-conformity to given mores, a thinking and living outside the box; call it defiant adventurism. Or like chameleons, we adapted to new environments.

Where and when did the Crazies begin? We know Thomas Briggs's wife Alice was a bit odd, or maybe just difficult, leading her grandson Robert to refer to her as 'the Briggs woman'. Could she have been the root of the craziness? She produced two daughters who in those days were certainly colourful. Helen could not have been too stable having had an abortion in 1906 while married. Surely that was a reckless decision to make as it had to be a back-street procedure, one I suspect she'd not shared beforehand with her husband Dana. Could it be she was having an affair? If nothing else, it showed a free-spirited unconventionality for a woman in those days. The Rhode Island *Pendulum* said she suffered from 'mental debility'.

As for Berenice, she wanted to get away from it all and so chose to run off with Major to Jamaica, where she painted, read horoscopes, had some shocking new flapper hairdo, and was referred to as the red witch. Just to have chosen to give up all the trappings of wealth, status, and predictable creature comfort in the US to take up an uncertain fate with a handsome rogue in a risky tropical isle shows, at the least, a reckless side.

Depression and suicide have plagued the family on all sides. Even on my mother's side there was alcoholism. My mother's father,

Norman Hastings, eventually succumbed to that disease. Major's father probably committed suicide in that ridiculous mongoose shooting accident, which a jury at the inquest ruled an accident, probably because it was just the easier outcome socially and for all concerned. Major's son from his second marriage to Enid, my half uncle Bob – actually named Harold Archer Melville after his father – was not of sound mind. He overdosed himself on Tofranil and died. And my brother Bryan also overdosed alone in a hotel room in New York on a business trip, his finances in ruin.

The saying goes that there's one in every family, but there are a whole heap in ours; some never worked or did anything productive, and only a few excelled. And what really marks the difference from all the other strands of my family is that the descendants of Thomas Briggs, through Helen and Berenice, would be to a certain extent protected from themselves for a while by the safety net of the trust money. Uncle Tom ended up in a mad house, yes, but eventually the family was able to get him into the best mental care facility money could buy. Jamaica ranks very low on the world suicide rate chart, and yet we have had three suicides in the family in as many generations. Maybe there was a curse on this family, not because of Briggs's money but because we are all fucking crazy!

But who am I to decide who the crazies are and what it takes to be judged crazy? How will others judge me? My life has had its crazy moments too. My Uncle Seymour, Harold's third son with his 'outside' family, proved to be an important person in my life. Growing up, my parents never admitted to me that he was related to us. I wonder who they thought they were protecting, me or themselves? What a fucked-up society we lived in! But I eventually learned the truth, and after my parents left Jamaica in the mid-1970s, I became close to my half uncle. He worked for the American mining company, Reynolds Jamaica Mines, which was close to our farm at Arthur's Seat. Seymour and his brothers became the only family I had left in Jamaica, as my own brothers had also gone. Seymour was the only one I knew very well; I knew Vincent casually when he came to Tropical Battery, and I never met Keith.

My father's brother from a different mother, five years younger than my dad, was born in 1920. I often wondered how it made him feel that his half-brother, my Dad, lived in the big house at Crescent with the man who was actually a father to them both, while he, his siblings, and his mother, Josephine Silvera, lived elsewhere, more humbly, on Crescent property. Seymour and I often met at a rum bar after work for a beer, and he was a regular visitor to our home, where my young children knew him as Uncle Seymour. If we had a curry-goat feed at the farm he would help me organize it. He was a good man and part of the fabric of my remaining family. We talked a lot about Major, and surprisingly Seymour showed no resentment towards his father. "He was not an easy man," he said simply. He was aware there were several other outside children.

It was Uncle Seymour, not my father, who took me up to Crescent to see the family home and my grandfather's grave. This is where Berenice and Major lived when she came to Jamaica in 1912. I was in my early thirties and seeing the grave for the first time. It was very emotional and brought home to me the monumental rift that seemed to have shaken our very concept of family. I can't say for sure if my dad attended his father's funeral in 1951, but he never felt the need to show me his father's final resting place. What a dysfunctional lot we are.

When I got back home to Ocho Rios that evening I got very drunk. I was angry and confused. Nothing seemed to make sense. I phoned my mum in Canada and picked a fight with her. It was a bad one; she didn't speak to me for months. I had grown up in

Jamaica as though with a single tap-root invested in this island as my home. My family as I knew it was that tap root, that sense of home, and now they were gone. But my Uncle Seymour, who had been mysteriously absent when I was growing up, was now my family in Jamaica and cared enough to take me to my grandfather's grave. What were these invisible lines that family refused to cross that kept us apart all those years? Jamaica was ruled by these senseless distinctions of legitimacy.

Those were not the only artificial distinctions; when I was very young people used to tell me I was born with a silver spoon in my mouth. This would piss me off, because it came over as an accusation of privilege that I never asked for, so why was I being made to feel uncomfortable? Growing up, I thought all Jamaican white people had money, played polo, lived in a world of comfort attended by an underclass of domestics, and gathered at all our social events. What I didn't realize back then was that many of them were not rich; they were at best middle class. But being white, or almost white, they enjoyed the privileges of upper-class colonial society, whereas wealthy black Jamaicans would struggle to join the club. These were my youthful perceptions of Jamaica's rich and poor.

Much of that has changed in today's Jamaica, largely due to the effects of the socialist '70s when legislative upheavals redefined both the economic and social realities with which we'd always lived. One of several pieces of social legislation the Michael Manley government enacted in the '70s was the Status of Children Act, which replaced the old colonial Bastard Act. The new Act provided equal status to all children irrespective of whether the father and mother were married. Prior to that, children born out of wedlock did not have the same rights of inheritance and civil rights as those within it, not to mention the social stigma of being referred to as a 'bastard'.

At the time these changes were taking place, I was facing similar upheaval in my family, an upheaval that may or may not have led to my two years, 1981 and 1982, of dissolute living after that harrowing decade ended: my very own 'crazy'. To explain how it all unfolded, it's necessary that I give you a snapshot of my immediate family. My Dad wasn't a lazy man, but he wasn't a businessman, that's for sure. He lived for his two sports, polo and bird shooting. Thinking about it now, I realize he really was a trust fund baby who never thought about making money; he just had it. From where I sit today and thinking back to some of the things my father did, like scouring the world markets for the best duck feed in preparation for shooting season, something he regarded as quite normal, I realize our family was far removed from reality. Thomas Briggs's money had made this possible.

Back then, my dad never invested in business in Jamaica, other than our properties: Arthur's Seat, the country home on the 500-acre hobby farm; Salt Island Estate, a splendid beach house in Discovery Bay on the north coast and a house in Kingston, which was later replaced with an apartment in Jamaica's first high-rise, Manor Court in Kingston.

Dad had inherited his money in the US and there it remained, in the same bank his grandfather used to set up the trust for his daughters. Like clockwork, every quarter a cheque came in the mail from Rhode Island. When my parents and all my siblings migrated to Canada in the 1970s, with the economy of not just Jamaica but of the wider world in shambles, our Jamaican companies that we had purchased over the previous eight years were in crisis. It was a perfect storm. In hindsight it all happened very quickly – a world recession in 1973 sparked by OPEC and the oil crisis, lack of confidence in the economy caused by socialist rhetoric at home, and infighting in the family that had forced my eldest brother, Bryan, out of the company – the Jamaican companies were suffering from absentee owners and no direction.

Bryan, almost ten years older than I, had left boarding school at Munro College in the late 1950s and went to Northeastern University in Boston where he studied business administration or 'Jewish Mechanics' as he called it back then, probably not realizing he had a fair amount of Jewish blood running through his veins, thanks to Major's mother. I believe he was a fairly good student, although I honestly don't remember if he graduated. What I know for sure is that he had a knack for business and while in Boston, he learned much about the family's wealth. Bryan was never the outdoor type. He never rode horses or went shooting like our father and when he returned to Jamaica after university, our dad bought him a car. Bryan became marketing manager at Stanley Motta, a large company that sold appliances in Kingston then moved to an advertising firm for a few years.

My brother Chris, three years younger than Bryan, was the opposite. He rode horses, was good at sports, was on the only school gymnastics team in Jamaica back then, and he enjoyed bird, skeet, and trap shooting. Chris wanted to become a vet and enrolled at Cornell University. That lasted about as long as a snowball in hell and back home he came. In about 1961, while still working for the advertising company in Kingston, Bryan encouraged Dad to buy a small fibreglass and plastics business, Marine and Plastics, and Christopher worked as the production manager. Nothing much came of that business and it was eventually either shut down or sold. Andrew, the third son, on the other hand, seemed to be a professional student. He trained to become an airline pilot in Florida but quit when he realized he was seriously colour blind.

He then studied hospitality somewhere in Europe, and I have lost track of what else, before returning to Jamaica to work in the family business.

Tragedy struck in 1962 when Chris had an accident playing polo. He was in a tournament with Dad in St Elizabeth on the south coast. My mother, Andrew, and I were there. Chris was twenty at the time and I was a few months shy of my 15th birthday. Chris went into a play, there was a hard bump with an opposing player – a 'ride off' to use the correct polo terminology – and his horse went down and then rolled over him, leaving him unconscious.

The Gilnoch polo field was in the middle of nowhere. The nearest town with a hospital of any size was in Mandeville, up in the hills, one-and-a-half hours away by car via an incredibly winding road known as Spur Tree Hill. There was no ambulance, not even a stretcher. We put down the two back seats of my father's nine-seater Ford station wagon, placed Chris carefully on a door removed from the bathroom of the tiny clubhouse, and put him in the wagon. My brother Andrew and I stayed with him in the back holding the door so it wouldn't slide around, and Dad took off at high speed for the hospital. It was the longest hour-and-a-half drive I've ever experienced, all while my older brother lay there unconscious. I remember repeatedly begging him to wake up as Dad sped up the winding road to the hospital.

Chris didn't wake up for three weeks and remained in hospital for three months. He'd suffered a brain injury, and we had to teach him to talk and walk. His recovery, as would be expected from a brain injury, was painfully slow. A few years later, even though he had recovered to a point, Dad recognized he would probably never do well in the corporate world so he bought Salt Island Estate, a 2,300-acre farm, South of Spanish Town, in the Hellshire area for Chris to manage. It was the opposite of the hilly Arthur's Seat property; it had a 300-acre lagoon and the land was dead flat, suitable for rice farming. There was also a dairy. In retrospect, I believe it was the lagoon that caught Dad's eye as it was filled with migratory ducks and teal that head south for the winter. I'm sure bells went off in my father's head! Now he would have two hunting seasons, the doves in the summer and ducks in the winter, and a lot of new best friends who were looking for an invite to hunt duck in the lagoon.

To attract more migratory ducks Dad realized he had to provide them with food, so he imported thousands of duck potato, wild celery, and other tubers from a wild game food nursery in the US and hand-planted these avian delicacies for them in the shallow lagoon. This seemed rather odd to many Jamaicans but was unremarkable to the family. 'Ducks Unlimited' would have been proud of Dad. After all, he'd made many a foray into the Trelawny 'bird bush' to uproot hundreds of *Bitter Damsel* and *Burnwood* plants to replant at Arthur's Seat to attract the white-winged doves and bald-pate pigeons by providing the berries and seeds they loved to eat. While the farm headman and I were trying to establish pastures for the herd of beef cattle, my dad was busy planting trees to feed the doves. Like the Arthur's Seat farm, Salt Island never turned a profit, and while two of my brothers never enjoyed hunting, the shooters in the family, Dad, Christopher and I, had a ball.

In the 1970s, Dad's greatest beef with the Michael Manley government came when the recession caused a spike in gun crime, and the administration's response was to limit the number of guns one person could own. My father had several, maybe ten, including a custom-fitted Belgian Browning 12-gauge over/under, with a walnut stock, beautiful engraving with gold inlay, and three sets of barrels. His guns were all sporting weapons, shotguns of varying gauges, rifles and pistols for target shooting; he never owned an assault-type weapon. He would spend hours every week oiling and cleaning them. After firing a gun he never put it away without cleaning it, and he made sure we never did, either. It was a familiar, beloved ritual to him. I imagine his dad taught him many of these things.

But to the government a gun was a gun, and the threat of having to give up his precious collection played a huge role in Dad's decision to leave Jamaica. All his siblings had left the island as soon as they came of age in the 1930s, probably to escape their father who was after their inheritance. John stayed in Jamaica and made his life and raised his family here. Now he was packing up to go to Vancouver, where he had already joined a skeet shooting club before he even had permanent residence in Canada.

Bryan, for his part, had entrepreneurial imagination. He had a vision to create an integrated automotive group of companies that involved manufacturing, distribution, and retail of everything automotive. So when Bostitch was finally sold in 1966, which had freed all the beneficiaries to use their money independently, Bryan encouraged Dad in 1967 to buy Tropical Battery Company Ltd, a manufacturer of automobile batteries, and a secondary lead smelter to recycle spent batteries. That was my father's first plunge into real business. The flagship, Tropical Battery, also operated thirteen small retail outlets across the island. Bryan went on a buying spree, adding an auto parts and accessories company, two large service stations, and a brake manufacturing company. The companies, mostly debt-financed by loans from local banks guaranteed by Dad's bank in Rhode Island, were under the umbrella of a holding company, Melcoe Ltd, with Dad serving as the chairman and Bryan

*Cameo of my grandmother
Berenice Briggs Melville*

*Dana's pocket watch with a photo of
Helen Briggs.*

Dorothy Lawrence and myself, Sarasota, Florida 2019

*My cousins Marianne Hirschman and her mother Helen
with me. Cape Cod, Massachusetts 2019*

L-R: Uncle Tom, Aunt Mary and Uncle Innis

Myself and cousin Pamela Melville McGregor, 2019

Polo in Victoria, British Columbia
L-R: Daniel Jr., Alexander, my mother Janet, Marc and me

Winsome Bowen Melville

Me and my boys. L-R: Daniel Jr., Marc and Alexander

*On the campaign trail with Councillor Eva Murdoch (L)
and a couple of constituents*

L-R: 'Aussie' Berenice, Aunt Mary and myself, Perth Australia, 2019

Aunt Alice's three children (L-R) Jacky, Joseph, 'Tahiti'
Berenice and myself, Papeete, Tahiti, 2019

*Briggs House, Arlington, Massachusetts built by my
great-grandfather in 1889*

*The garage at the back of the Briggs's house (renovated) where my
great-grandfather made several of his inventions*

My Uncle Tom and Lucille Parks (Iremonger)
circa 1933

Me in 1982

Ma and Pops hugging

Ma and myself

Ma and her friend Toni

Dogsled Days:
L-R: Jimmy Buffett, Newton
Marshall, Chris Blackwell,
Danny 2005

Carole and I in Barbados, March 2020

Introducing

Daniel Archer "Danny" Melville J.P.

PNP
Candidate for
North East
St. Ann

PNP

Campaign brochure 1997

Carole and I at my 60th
birthday party

Danny and Carole's Wedding Day

L-R (back): Alexander, Nikola, Danny, Carole, Rachel, Alexander, Daniel, Marc. (Front row) Erica, Thomas.

May 1994

as managing director. It was owned entirely by the family. Should this loan default, this wouldn't have wiped Dad out but it would have put a serious dent in his finances.

Things fell apart relatively quickly. We had only been in business in Jamaica for about eight years when, with the recession creating havoc, Bryan, then CEO of the group was forced out, and family members began fleeing the island. In the fire sale that took place as Jamaicans fled in the mid-1970s, my father sold all his properties for cents in the dollar – Arthur's Seat, the 2,300-acre Salt Island Estate, the beach house, and a luxurious Manor Court apartment in Kingston. He lost a ton of money on these fire sales on top of his business losses. He sold one company for the debt he owed the bank – it was worth three times that amount. Walking away from Jamaica cost him millions in money and in lost opportunity.

A good friend who knew a little about our family's connection with Bostitch once asked me: "Do you know how to make a small fortune in Jamaica?" "How?" I asked. "Start with a big one and piss it away," he replied.

Life in families, even the best of them, is often like Greek tragedy. Greed and jealousy had set in among us siblings, and Dad didn't know how to deal with it. We had all been spoilt from an early age. We wanted for nothing; we had each been given a car when we learned to drive and a house when we got married. Each brother complained that the other drove a more expensive car, or had a bigger house, or was making more money. Writing to his sister Alice in 1971, a note of exasperation was evident in Dad's comment that, "My role as father of four spirited sons has not been easy either." Dad's 'either' was probably a response to some reference of Alice to a recent carefree spending spree of her three equally spirited children.

Now we were all spread out: me in Jamaica, my parents in Vancouver, and later Victoria British Columbia, Bryan was living in Vancouver, as was Andrew, and Chris was in Toronto. In 1975 tragedy struck the family again when Bryan committed suicide in New York. He was thirty-seven years old. My mother was devastated and never really got over it. Bryan had mailed a suicide letter from New York to my father in Canada, which obviously arrived after he died. He had suffered from depression and had financial problems. Who knows what else, what desperation, contributes to such a rash and tragic decision.

When I look back on that tragedy, it was a terrible time for my parents. At their age, to lose their properties, their businesses, a son, a country... having to start from scratch to build a new home was almost too much. But for any Jamaican, the 1970s was a time of such revolutionary change, socially, economically, and spiritually. One could almost say that Jamaica, unique and fiercely independent-minded, rebellious by nature – just listen to its music – had caught a good dose of the crazies too.

After everyone had left Jamaica I got involved with the companies in Kingston. The brake company was sold for the debt, the service stations were closed and I was able to refinance the core company, Tropical Battery, and release my Dad's personal US-dollar guarantees in Rhode Island, literally saving him a few million dollars. My father was well pleased and rewarded me well. I felt invincible. And that's when I screwed up big time.

It was by now the 1980s. My wife and three sons were living in the US. I was flying to Miami for about a week every month to see them, but otherwise I was in Jamaica on my own, missing my boys. By now the whole family had gone – I guess there was no anchor or wise advice to be had, and to be honest I felt a certain amount of anger and resentment about the family running off and leaving our homeland. But I make no excuses; I just offer this as background to my life at the time. I got in with a fast crowd, and the 'white lady', cocaine. I'm compulsive by nature. I dived in head first; it was after all an easy 'out' from reality or responsibility, a way of ignoring how I was feeling. It took about two years for me to come to my senses.

But in that crazy time I made bad decisions. I was living what felt like a double life: about a week a month in Florida, then back to Jamaica. Credit was easy in Florida and so using the 'reward' Dad had given me, I leveraged real estate there. When the crash of 1981 hit and the bottom fell out of the real estate market, I went flat broke. I couldn't make the mortgage payments or get tenants for the rental properties and had to 'fire-sale' the real estate. I lost a ton of money but still had Tropical Battery and the Jamaican assets to fall back on. I remember going to Dad cap in hand, and he gave me a small bail-out to mop up some personal bills in Florida. I told him the truth about the drugs; he was disgusted with me. So five years after bailing out my Dad, it was I who had needed a bailout.

I believe the realization that I could actually go broke was my incentive to quit cocaine. I stopped cold turkey, none of this 'my name is Danny and I'm a drug addict' group therapy for me, no rehab of any kind. It was tough at first. I had already bought the fifty acres of land on the ocean at Chukka Cove to build the equestrian and polo facility, so I retreated there, leaving a manager to run the battery company in Kingston. I spent my days doing manual labour; I would spend hours driving the tractor and cutting the polo field with a gang mower, back and forth. I'd brush cut the horse pastures, plant fence posts, ride horses. I distanced myself from the coke crowd for fear of backsliding and smoked a lot of weed. In fact, I swear the weed helped me stay off the hard drugs. So much for ganja being blamed as a gateway drug – it was my gateway out.

After quitting the hard drugs, I was back to spending a few days a week in the battery business in Kingston and working the rest of the week at Chukka Cove. Looking back, it was such a chaotic time, all happening in just three and a half years: Winsome and the kids moved to Florida in early 1980, my crazy sex, drugs, and Negril years were 1981 and '82, and then by 1983 Winsome and the kids were back home. Chukka Cove opened in March 1983. Winsome and I were then separated, though we wouldn't get divorced for another four years. The kids went to school in Kingston, but they came to Chukka Cove every weekend and all school holidays, riding and doing chores at the farm. That continuity probably accounts for the very close relationship I have with my three boys to this day.

I then met Yvonne Whittingham, who eventually became my second wife. Yvonne was an excellent riding instructor excelling in dressage, show-jumping, and three-day eventing. She took over the reins, so to speak, at Chukka Cove and organized the horse shows and other equestrian events. She taught my sons, and a host of other young girls and boys, to ride. We played a lot of polo, often taking the horses to the beach afterwards for a swim which the kids loved. Yvonne organized Pony Club camps in the summer whereby twenty or more kids and young teenagers from Kingston would sleep on mattresses on the floor at the stables. In the days they learned to muck stalls – shovel horseshit – and groom horses. They took riding lessons and went on group out-rides up into the hills. In the afternoons everyone would go to the cliffs and jump into the ocean to cool off and frolic in the bat cave.

At first Yvonne and I lived together in a tiny apartment attached to the stables; one couldn't get any closer to the horses. As an equestrian centre Chukka Cove was not making a lot of money and we worked with our horses in a couple of movie productions that paid well, staging period polo tournaments and doing horse and carriage work for a Disney mini-series, *Return to Treasure Island*. Thinking back on it now, it was a glorious time to be alive.

One of the most rewarding activities we undertook at Chukka Cove in the 1980s was a riding programme for underprivileged children with intellectual disabilities. The therapeutic value of horseback riding for mentally and physically challenged children is well known worldwide. Unfortunately, children with disabilities are sometimes looked down upon, so it was wonderful to reverse that view for our riders, for them to be on top of and in control of so powerful a beast, to look down at the world, if only for a couple of hours a week.

The kids came to Chukka Cove three times a week for riding lessons with Yvonne. We got involved with the Jamaica Special Olympics and formed an equestrian team under their umbrella. We raised money and after a couple of years we took two of our riders as part of the larger Jamaican contingent to the 1987 Special Games at Notre Dame University in South Bend, Indiana. It was an incredible experience, with the Jamaican team winning several medals in multiple disciplines, including equestrian. One of the highlights of the games was the opening ceremony held in the famous Notre Dame football stadium. The stadium, including the infield, was packed to capacity with athletes, coaches, family friends, and locals, who all came out to show their support. When the glorious Whitney Houston appeared on the stage to sing a couple of songs including her iconic hit, *Didn't We Almost Have It*

All, there wasn't a dry eye in the 60,000-seat stadium. To see the expressions on our athletes' faces, these kids from Jamaica, as they took in the sights and sounds in that arena made the programme worthwhile.

The riding programme continued at the farm and four years later we attended the games in Minneapolis-St Paul in 1991. There we met Eunice Shriver, the founder of Special Olympics, who spent a lifetime working on behalf of the disabled.

Unfortunately, the crazy gene in me surfaced again and ten years after Yvonne and I got together it was over. I had an affair that had disastrous consequences. Was I any different than my grandfather? I asked Rachel that question recently. Her reply: "You both had the crazy gene but your grandfather lacked insight and integrity. You don't." I hope she's right.

18

Walking the Walk with Carole

I met Carole Anne Brennan when we were teenagers in Jamaica. She had gone to live with the Manleys at Rachel's invitation. Carole and Rachel were school friends and after Carole's dad, a senior banker with Barclays Bank, had been transferred to Barbados with the family, Carole wanted to finish high school in Jamaica.

Back in the 1960s we had our little gang of teenagers that hung out together, at the beach, at parties, the usual stuff adolescents do. I developed a terrible crush on Carole, which had amounted to nothing as she left Jamaica upon graduating high school. Rachel and Carole remained lifelong friends, but I never laid eyes on her for another twenty-eight years. Life went on, she got married and had five children and I got married twice and had three. Fast forward to the end of 1992, and my second marriage was on the rocks while Carole had separated from her husband in Barbados. Rachel encouraged Carole to pay her a visit in Jamaica, where we met again and that was it: the crush was renewed, this time on both sides. It turned swiftly to love, and we have been together ever since.

You could say we are polar opposites; she's an Aquarian and I'm a Libran. I don't really put much stock in astrology, and yet I find myself light-heartedly referring to it, so maybe it's a nod to my grandmother and to Tahiti Berenice. Free-spirited and eccentric, Aquarians, they say, can often be identified by their offbeat fashion sensibilities, unusual hobbies, and non-conformist attitude. Aquarius is ruled by Uranus, the planet of ultra-progressive thinking that governs innovation, technology, change, and reform. Aquarians are said to be very private. My wife is all these things. She is quiet, calm, soft-spoken, tolerant – and stubborn as hell. To me, she's the kind of person who, if she's on my side, somehow I know I'll be okay. Artistic and creative, she is conversely fascinated by anything technological – the latest camera or gadget – and if you give her a problem to solve, she is great at figuring out the logistics. Carole also likes to potter. At first you might think she's just fiddling around, but you will discover that with her endless capacity for patience and concentration, she is usually creating something – a painting of a tree through a window, with each of a thousand separate tiny leaves visible. Or a portrait of her father's ancient caretaker, or one of her grandchildren – she has thirteen. Or, she's refurbishing, redecorating some room of our home.

Libra is an air sign, which is supposed to mean I am cool, calculating, cerebral, and charming. We are said to possess a natural surface cleverness and swift humour that make us good company. Librans are best known for our love of balance; being an air sign, Libra is filled to the brim with romantic thoughts, and loves to share them. We are supposed to have a soft, gentle, and non-threatening Venusian vibe, with great taste in fashion and art, to boot. We usually move in a graceful way, but when the balance is off, it is off.

Well, that last question of balance itself is off when it comes to me. Because my feet are afflicted with a genetic condition, at my best I stumble along! I am certainly not graceful. And I am a romantic who falls madly in love, but I'm not always a confident person. I'm not sure about the good taste in clothes – Carole buys them all for me! If cerebral means I live in my head, that's probably true as I never stop thinking and that's probably what gets me into trouble. But I'm not at all intellectual or academic.

The sum total works. Carole is my ballast. I have all these bright ideas and Carole makes them work. She is the most practical person. And she's patient, which is probably the main reason that we are able to walk that walk together. Most of all she has a sense of humour, and when I'm not being moody, we have a good laugh at life together.

Carole and I got married in 1994 and slowly and with care and love on both sides amalgamated the two families of us and eight children. Shortly before we got married, Carole organized a grand family reunion in the summer of 1993 at my seaside home 'Limetree' in Ocho Rios. My three sons and her five, three girls and two boys in Barbados all congregated in the large home which over-flowed with a summer of laughter and fun, eating and drinking, my boys doing their customary dives from the roof of the house into the pool where the kids swam and played endless games of dominoes, a table submerged in the water at the shallow end. Special friendships were formed. This holiday was Carole's brainwave. Sometimes these situations can be difficult, but the young are adaptable and bond especially when there's fun going down, and this holiday laid the basis for what has become a close and comfortable blended family.

Limetree Villa was sold, but we all remember that special, priceless summer forever captured on tape by Carole's eldest daughter, Nikola, who was studying film at the time, in spite of the annoyance that her constant filming caused.

***

I've always loved politics but never actually thought of running for an office before I met Carole. Instead, I did my part in nation building through public service. My first stint was chairing the government-owned thoroughbred horse racing promoting company Caymanas Park for several years. Working with the sometimes-fractious racing associations, the grooms, trainers, owners and breeders we modernized the industry and had great success turning around the fortunes at the track from bankruptcy.

Many people say the racetrack is a microcosm of the Jamaican society. In a little story that gives insight into our psyche and sometimes the Anancy in us – Anancy being a good-natured, innovatively scheming, and irrepressible trickster spider of Jamaican folklore. Once while I was talking with a trainer known for manipulating the occasional race, he explained to me: "Danny winning a race is great, but the winning is really sweet when a little racket is involved." To him the thrill of beating the system was what it was all about.

In my hometown of Ocho Rios, because of my association with tourism I was asked to chair the government corporation that managed the world-famous Dunn's River Falls and Park and other government-owned assets and attractions in St Ann parish. I moved from this after three years to head up another government agency mandated to enhance the tourism product in Jamaica.

Then the crazy gene hit again. In the early summer of 1997, the PNP asked me to contest the seat in the St Ann North East constituency in the upcoming general election. The constituency included the resort town of Ocho Rios and the parish capital St

Ann's Bay, and a large rural hilly area dotted with small villages and subsistence farmers. I knew the area well as I grew up in the hills and had worked and campaigned for other candidates over the years.

I discussed the idea of running with Carole and my boys, as they would now have to step up and take full control of the battery company and my tourism-based business, Chukka, while I went on this wild ride. They agreed. Carole was ready! And what a campaigner she turned out to be, not just talking the talk, but also walking the walk. We started in June and for six months we campaigned house to house. My small team of handlers, all veterans of earlier campaigns and local area leaders, mapped out our itinerary. By the time the date of the election was finally announced we had covered every nook and cranny of the constituency, and Carole had a huge following of women whose every need – from clothes and school books for their children to sewing machines she begged from local businesses – she found a way to fulfil. I was running, planning the campaign to win the constituents' minds, while my always generous wife was quietly, one by one, winning their hearts.

The last four or five weeks before polling day in December were exhausting. We'd start each morning with a strategy meeting of the campaign committee and end with three public meetings at night, hammering the same talking points in villages and towns across the constituency. Jamaicans are big on funerals and wakes and the candidate has to be seen at every funeral if you hope to win, it's part of our culture. Not a church-goer myself, my baptism of fire was at a service in a tiny town, New Ground in Lime Hall, when the pastor likened me to Daniel in the lion's den, and Carole and I were duly anointed with oil as the congregation 'tek the spirit' with startling enthusiasm as they were instructed by their spiritual leader whom to vote for.

When my campaign manager got wind that a party supporter had died in Great Pond, a residential suburb of Ocho Rios, the team went into action. He reached out to the pastor of the evangelical church, who had connections with the local taxi drivers' union. I had helped the taxi association some twenty years earlier, when they were organizing themselves into a co-op, providing them an office rent-free for a number of years, and they remembered that. The funeral was on a Saturday afternoon in August. As I saw the church, I recognized the building as a popular but short-lived nightclub called The Spanish Main, where I'd partied a few times in the late '60s.

It was incredibly hot, even for Jamaica, and the church was packed to overflowing as the deceased was a prominent member of the community. We knew that both my opponents would not miss an opportunity to be seen at a funeral, with many hundreds of voters from the area. As my opponents sat like sardines in a packed pew in sweltering heat with the congregation, I arrived fashionably late and was whisked around to the back of the church and made a grand entrance onto the platform where the pastors and a visiting bishop were seated. Comfortable swivel armchairs were provided for Carole and I, with me sitting directly beside the bishop. I looked down at the congregation, saw my political opponents and gave them a smug smile and a little wave. Everything was going well as pastor after pastor waxed lyrical about the Lord, the need for everyone to come to Jesus, and the dear departed who had been a pillar of the church. There were the usual slowly droned hymns building on and up and moments of joyous hand-clapping.

Then, disaster.

The presiding pastor, who also owned a taxi, proceeded to tell the congregation that 'the Member of Parliament in waiting' – a direct instruction to the congregation as to who they should vote for in the upcoming election – was here and was going to speak about the dear departed. That's when I panicked; my team had forgotten to brief me about the life of the deceased! I didn't even know his name. I had nowhere to run, no solution to reach for – not even Carole could save me now – so I stood up and walked to the edge of the platform, took a long look down at the body in the open coffin with one last hope that I would recognize the fellow. I didn't.

I started to speak and after a few general references to the 'dear departed' I was really sweating; I put my hand to my forehead and faked a slight stagger pretending that I was overcome with grief. With one accord the entire congregation went '*Ooohhhh*'. One of the pastors rushed up to me and guided me slowly back to my comfortable chair while the presiding pastor explained to the faithful that I was indeed overcome with grief. One of the church sisters was immediately delegated to fan me for the rest of the service, which she did using her elaborately filigreed granny fan.

There's one other funeral story I'd like to share. Winning the election which I did, and becoming the member of parliament meant you had to attend the funerals. The MP's attendance is mandatory, part of our political culture, and Carole and I attended as many as possible. I remember one in particular that was taking place in the tiny village of Beecher Town in the hills of the constituency. The village was close to where I grew up, so this time I knew the family of the deceased, as I did the majority of the villagers. He was a young man who was living in New York, where he had been shot and killed. The family had gone to great expense to ship the body in an expensive white casket to Jamaica so he could be laid to rest in the land of his birth; cremation is not an option for Jamaican country folk, they believe in burying the body, not the ashes.

Apart from paying respects and offering sympathy to the family of the deceased, funerals are a wonderful opportunity for a member of parliament to catch up with constituents and press the flesh, so Carole and I arrived well before the 4:00 p.m. start time. We mingled with the crowd outside the beautiful little cut-stone church and waited, and waited, for the hearse to arrive. Eventually a small beat-up pickup truck arrived in a cloud of dust with the white coffin hanging out the back. The widow had paid for a hearse, not a pickup, and very quickly her embarrassment turned to anger. There was much shouting and colourful language before we eventually found out what had gone wrong. The funeral home had two burials that fateful afternoon but only one hearse. Their plan was to drop off one body at the first funeral and then rendezvous with the pickup, which was carrying 'our' casket at a point close to the church, transfer the coffin to the hearse and make a grand entrance. But the driver of the hearse lost his way on the network of narrow winding country roads, all devoid of directional signs, and was unable to link up with the truck to make the switch. The pickup driver, realizing he was now very late for the funeral, decided he better deliver the body to the church.

In the panic that ensued and to the horror of the family and congregants in the packed church, the pickup driver, now acting as the funeral director, wheeled the coffin into the church head first, a cardinal sin unless the deceased is a pastor, and this set off another round of condemnation from family and friends. As a result, the coffin which couldn't be turned in the aisle had to be reversed out and then turned around to be brought into the church the correct way. The service went ahead without further incident, and I gave a short address to the bereaved family. On this occasion, I knew exactly who had died.

Then came the interment in the church yard. The family had built a vault of concrete blocks to receive the casket. Everyone assembled graveside and to the horror of all, the coffin could not fit in the grave; the fancy white American casket was wider than a standard Jamaican one. The event was now running hopelessly behind schedule, long shadows were stretching across the church yard, and traditionally in Jamaica, relic from the days of slavery, funerals had to be over by sunset. And so, with the sun sinking behind the green hills of St Ann, we all stood at the graveside rejoicing to the Lord and singing hymn after hymn, while grave diggers frantically used pickaxes and sledge hammers to break the concrete and widen the hole so the coffin could be lowered. It was a photo-finish.

I had won my seat comfortably however the party also won big so there was an abundance of the old boys available for the cabinet and no room for a newcomer. Even with my experience in tourism I was relegated to the back bench. Rather than being in a position to shape policy for the country, particularly in tourism, I would be handing out scarce benefits and spoils to an army of constituents seeking some form of help for whatever their personal problems were. Pure pork barrel politics. In retrospect I should have cut a back-room deal for a position in the Tourism Ministry *before* I agreed to contest the seat.

After the initial euphoria wore off, I realized that what I enjoyed about politics was the campaigning and not retail politics handing out zinc and plywood to constituents in need of a shanty. I was an idealist. I had this dream of helping to shape policy, bringing new ideas to the national table, making a difference to my country. I became totally frustrated and resigned after three years of my five-year term. In my public statement I explained:

My role as parliamentarian seems to be defined as an attender of funerals, a coordinator of patronage and a symbol of tribalism... I find I can no longer be part of a system that glorifies mediocrity and denigrates any vision of excellence. ...I began in 1997 with hope. And sadly I have ended with disillusionment...My deep sadness is that I have not been able to deliver to the good people of N.E. St. Ann the dreams and hopes that inspired my desire to serve.

With that, I had embarrassed the government and I was now a pariah in the political party I had supported for decades. It really hurt. But it was water under the bridge. We'll always have our differences, but it's still my party.

It's said that you can't keep a good man down. I don't know about that, but I'd say you can't always subdue a crazy one. When I'd done licking my wounds, I was on to a new challenge. I guess when I couldn't be creative in government I still tried through my Chukka tour company now run by my sons to find interesting new ways to promote my country, share its unique idiosyncrasies with the ever curious flow of tourists, and create employment and prosperity. In the tour business, to ensure a competitive edge, one needs to dream up and develop new tours and attractions. Here was my opportunity for crazy.

At Chukka Cove I dreamed up the idea of the Zion bus in 2002. I wanted to provide an experience that took cruise passengers who were hardcore Bob Marley and reggae disciples, in a themed retro Jamaican 'country bus' with no air-conditioning and reggae music booming from six bass speakers deep into the mountains of St Ann to the village of Nine Mile, to the house where Bob Marley was born and spent the first twelve years of his life. It is both his birthplace and final resting place.

The Zion bus is all the creation of our dear friend and artist Zoda assisted by Carole. They painted and decorated the inside of an old, abandoned bus, transforming it into the visual world of Bob Marley with hundreds of pictures and memorabilia plastered over it. And the strange thing is, Carole being Carole, she would emerge from the bus many hours later in her typical blue jeans and T-shirt as the light was fading with not so much as a splash on her clothes! As with the politics, my long-suffering wife was there beside me, her practical bent making my crazy possible.

My most treasured memory setting up the tour was driving to Nine Mile where I met with Bob's mum Cedella Booker, who was by then very old. She was salt of the earth, an old country woman with timeless eyes, the kind that know the past and know the future. She was a vegetarian and still very sprightly. We smoked a joint together in her home. I felt as though I was anointed. Sadly, she would die about five years later.

Fast forward twenty years and every day there are a few Zion busses carrying happy visitors on the route from Ocho Rios to Nine Mile to pay homage to Marley. Thousands of reggae fans make the pilgrimage on the incredibly narrow, winding road up to Nine Mile every year, using private cars and taxis. But there is only one Zion Bus Line. The Zion bus with its driver and a DJ playing reggae while telling Bob's life story is a huge part of the overall tour experience. And I believe it's better to take passengers to Nine Mile where they can have a smoke than to have them wandering around the market and back streets of Ocho Rios looking for weed, getting ripped off, seriously harassed, and occasionally even mugged.

One of my more spectacular failures was, believe it or not, related to my love of reggae. I have known Michael Butler, the American theatrical producer now in his nineties, for about forty years. He used to bring a polo team to Jamaica every winter and we would take a team to his Oak Brook Polo Club every summer; it became an annual polo exchange. Michael's father, Paul Butler, had transformed the family dairy farm into the village of Oak Brook, one of metropolitan Chicago's best-known western suburbs. Being an avid polo player, Paul Butler also founded the Oak Brook Polo Club, one of America's oldest, in 1922.

Michael was one hell of a promoter and hosted Jamaica Day at Oak Brook Polo Club, an event that ran annually for several years and became a hit which drew the largest crowd of the season. With the Jamaica Tourist Board and Red Stripe on board as major sponsors, the party after the final match under the big tent field-side always featured a reggae band with dancing and libations continuing into the night.

If America was a monarchy and not a republic, Michael would definitely be one of her princes. He is descended from old Midwest money, sailed with Jack Kennedy, and his exploits – including successes and failures – would fill an encyclopaedia. He once admitted to affairs with both Audrey Hepburn and Rock Hudson! He is probably best known as the producer of the 1960s tribal love-rock musical *Hair*, and of course playing the noble sport of polo. His politics are liberal, and he was proud of making Richard Nixon's 'Enemies List,' twice.

Michael lived by the philosophy that it's 'better to be looked over than overlooked'. Known as the hippie millionaire, he produced several other shows and a few movies. Self-admittedly not the best manager of money, he went bankrupt in 1991. He blames the customary family fight over money for his fall from grace but one could never say Michael lived inexpensively; he always had an entourage of hangers on, and if anything he was too kind.

So, in 1993 when a mutual friend, Jamaica's most talented architect, blues club and restaurant owner, Evan Williams, approached me to invest in a gospel-reggae musical production called 'Revelations', which would have Michael Butler as its executive producer, how could I refuse? Michael was broke, but he certainly had the experience and connections to be a facilitator for such a venture. Always willing to support anything reggae, I dived in head first – again.

Michael brought in Chapman Roberts as director. Chapman had been a member of the cast in the original Broadway production of *Hair* and is an acclaimed vocal arranger and musical director, director and producer, on and off Broadway. A cast of some of the best voices in Jamaica was assembled, a large hall was rented, and rehearsals began in earnest. It was a big production and Chapman flew in from NYC for weeks at a time to work. Watching him work with an all-Jamaican cast was inspirational. Michael also made several trips to Jamaica to oversee the production. The show was a huge undertaking with a large cast and impressive set. The premiere would be held in Jamaica and the production would move to the US if it was successful, Broadway maybe; is there anything wrong with dreaming big?

The Ranny Williams Entertainment Centre in Kingston, where the show would take place, is an outdoor venue. There were two performances, one each night, over the weekend. The production was underfunded from the outset, but everyone was excited and put in the extra effort, as no show like this had been attempted in Jamaica before. There was a mad rush to the finish line and when opening night arrived the set looked amazing, even though it was obvious to many it was not one hundred per cent complete. However, the weekend weather report was predicting inclement weather due to a low-pressure system over Jamaica. Though it rained most of the day, many ticket holders turned up with raincoats. The show must go on, and so it did. It pretty much rained throughout the entire performance, and also the next day and night of the second performance. All that moisture played havoc with the sound, adding to what would prove a disaster.

'Revelations' was an undeserved flop because the music was first-class and all original. An uplifting show, under different circumstances it may have been a success. It was heartbreaking, after all that time, effort and investment, to be rained out both nights. Still, there were people who loved the show and expressed support for our valiant attempt at producing the world's first gospel-reggae musical for the stage. Carole had been fully involved, attending rehearsals with me and offering encouragement, and she was there to commiserate when the rain came pouring down on our parade!

Talk about the crazy gene. Not one of my better investments. Instead of the satisfaction of a smash hit, what I ended up with was a stack of contract documents and agreements six inches thick. They sat in my desk drawer for several years before I finally chucked them. But sometimes I console myself with the memory of Don Quixote's impossible dream as he tilted at windmills. Maybe one day, my passions – successes, even the partial ones, and all my near misses – will themselves inspire a musical hit!

My next mad venture was the Jamaica Dogsled Team. I had been on a business trip to Edmonton, Alberta, to look at dune buggies for our tourism business when I spotted a cart with wheels on the compound. I was told by the owner that it was a cart for the equivalent of dog sledding but on dry land. I discovered that this was an established sport that had yearly races in places where there was no snow.

Jamaica has no snow and Jamaica has thousands of homeless mongrels, stray dogs with no owners and no purpose. It didn't take me long to figure out a new attraction and tour for Chukka Cove. It was 2005 and I dreamed up the insane idea to develop a dogsled tour – that's right, dogsled, not bobsled for which the Jamaican team became famous when they entered the Calgary Winter Olympics in 1988 and inspired the classic Disney comedy *Cool Runnings*, starring John Candy. I suspected 'dogsled' would play well with 'bobsled', and it did.

My idea was to create a short dry-land tour using rescued mongrels pulling a 'sled' with wheels at Chukka Cove while at the same time promoting the company and Jamaica's tourism by taking young mushers to train and race in Alaska and the Yukon Territory. My family and many friends thought I'd lost my mind yet again! Carole rolled her eyes.

I also recognized the cost of racing overseas was going to be prohibitive and that I needed sponsorship. On a chance meeting with Jimmy Buffett, who happened to be visiting Jamaica, I realized while talking to him over lunch that he just might be crazy enough to share my vision of seeing Jamaicans compete in yet another winter sport. It was a long shot so I just blurted it out at the dining table: "Jimmy, I want to start a dogsled team." Most of the people around the table choked on their food, but Jimmy's response was, "I love it and want to be a part of it." Jimmy said he had missed out on the Jamaica Bobsled Team years before and he wasn't going to miss out on this one. Once we had Jimmy on board we were able to attract a few minor sponsors to help defray the cost.

Jimmy has always had a special love for Jamaica. His interest and love had been tested some years earlier when he landed his seaplane in the waters off the cliffs of Negril and a wanna-be Rambo policeman assumed it was a ganja plane coming for a load of weed and shot at him, putting a few holes in the fuselage. All hell broke loose subsequently, and the Jamaican government offered him an apology. Most people would have let that be their last visit to the island; not Jimmy. He took it in stride, wrote a song called *Jamaica Mistaica* about the incident and sold another couple of million records.

And so it was that the Jamaica Dogsled Team was born and nobody was laughing at me anymore. We knew nothing about the sport, and with the sponsorship of Jimmy's restaurant chain, Margaritaville, we brought Alan Stewart, a musher from Scotland, and Rick Johnson from Minnesota, to help us train our mutts, set up the kennel at Chukka Cove and teach Jamaicans how to train and care for the dogs.

True to form, rushing in where angels would fear to tread, the project fast becoming an obsession with me, we set up two teams for racing overseas, our sprint team coached by Minnesota musher Ken Davis. Ken drove his Jamaica Dogsled Team-branded truck loaded with dogs – dubbed the 'Sun Dogs'. Also on board were harnesses, kibble, two light racing sleds strapped on top, and a young Jamaican musher; they travelled hundreds of miles across Minnesota and Michigan in the US, and Ontario in Canada, entering a different sprint race in a local town every weekend.

At the same time, we had our eye on running the legendary Iditarod and the Yukon Quest, two 1,000-mile sled-dog races across some of the most inhospitable terrain on the planet. Both these races are actually wilderness survival experiences that take about ten days to complete and can be very dangerous for the mushers and their dogs as temperatures can drop to -40° Celsius. Everything from frostbite to the sled and musher falling through thin ice into a lake or river is in play. This is serious stuff. Just completing these races is considered a victory as a great percentage of mushers are forced to withdraw from the race for one reason or another.

A brave young Jamaican named Newton Marshall, who'd never left the island much less seen snow, was chosen. It would take several winters with leased Alaskan husky dog teams and champion mushers like Hans Gatt in Whitehorse, Yukon, and one of the greatest mushers of all time, Lance Mackey, in Anchorage, Alaska, to train and prepare this Jamaican kid to survive on the trail and hopefully finish the race. These two races are considered so tough that to qualify a musher has to have completed at least one 200-mile and one 300-mile accredited race beforehand. Newton qualified and in February 2009 we ran the Yukon Quest, the first 1,000-mile race; it runs from Whitehorse, Yukon, to Fairbanks, Alaska. The Quest is as tough, some say tougher, as the Iditarod but not as well known.

In March 2010 we were finally ready to run the Iditarod. A freezing Newton on the trail made this classic statement with a big smile on his face: "This is no way for a black man to die." And even though he was way down on the list of finishers, every person in the small town of Nome came out to greet him when he did; it was as if he had won the race. One guy had a huge sign that read, "There's a new Marshall in town and his name is Newton," in obvious reference to Wyatt Earp, the deputy marshal who moved to Nome with the 1899 gold rush and ran a saloon and brothel.

Jimmy Buffett took a great interest in Newton and his team and used to follow the longer races on the official websites, tracking Newton for a thousand miles from Anchorage to Nome. Over the course of seven or eight years, Newton and the team became quite famous. He did countless TV interviews and specials. Chris Blackwell, a friend of Jimmy who produced Bob Marley's music and owned Island Records, produced a documentary, *Sun Dogs*, about the team. Then a book was written by Whitehorse author

John Firth, called *One Mush*, and a second documentary on the story was made called *Underdog*. A third documentary chronicling Newton's Iditarod run was also made but never released.

All good things must come to an end, and having completed the world's two toughest sled-dog races and with sponsorship slipping, we decided to retire the team and call it a day – but not before finding good homes for all our rescued Sun Dogs back in Jamaica. Over those seven or eight years, Carole and I travelled thousands of miles across the vast wilderness of the Far North, visiting the Yukon Territory six times and Alaska five. We fell in love with Dawson City, the heritage town built at the time of the Klondike gold rush where I had the famous Sour Toe Cocktail, a rite of passage in Dawson. The drink consists of a shot of whisky with a mummified human toe in it. One must drink the whisky and kiss the toe.

Another favourite town for me was Nome, Alaska, where the Iditarod ends and where the Old West lawman Wyatt Earp ran a saloon and made a small fortune during the Nome Gold Rush of 1899. I met several wonderful people and learned a few of the ways of the Far North, memories I will hold dear until I die.

One of the first people we met in Whitehorse Yukon Territory was Richard 'Dick' Watts. Dick was the only optometrist in town. He opened his home to us. He knew everyone. Dick had a lifelong love affair with Jamaica and eventually sold his business, followed his heart and moved there. Ironically, he now lives on a property opposite to my grandfather's family home at Cresent, St Mary.

Every step of the way, through northern wilderness and freezing temperatures, Carole was faithfully there beside me immortalizing my venture for the records with the thousands of photographs she took. Maybe she's got the crazy gene too.

Over those years, Newton and the rest of the team became quite famous, and he did countless TV interviews and specials. Jimmy Buffett took a great interest in him and his team as well. In November 2009 Jimmy was giving a concert in Toronto. Newton was also in town as we were holding a fund-raiser for the dogsled team over that same weekend. Tickets for Jimmy's show were organized, and we got to the concert early so we could go backstage and catch up with him. After the mandatory PR photos with Newton, we were about to go out front when Jimmy said he had a surprise for Newton and we should listen up for it.

About halfway through the concert Jimmy gave Newton and the Jamaica Dogsled Team a huge shout out, telling the 20,000 'Parrotheads', as Buffett fans are called, that Newton Marshall, the Jamaican musher, was in the house and was on his way to Alaska to run the Iditarod. The crowd cheered. Jimmy then proceeded to sing an inspirational song he had recently released called 'Wings'. It was the first live performance of the song. It's a song about everybody having a pair of wings 'that you can't see', that everybody can actually fly if 'you'd just take another point of view'. In the last verse he inserted Newton and sang, 'You have wings you can't see, silver wings like Newton and me...'. The crowd went wild. Newton was beaming. It was a fitting song for a kid from Jamaica about to attempt to run the Last Great Race on Earth.

At the end of the show, it took us forever to get out of the arena, and everybody who saw Newton wanted a photo taken with him. Jimmy's Parrothead fans have to be some of the most devoted and unique in the world; they come to his concerts dressed in parrot headgear, masks, plumes of feathers, and the strangest costumes. It was a wonderful show. Carole, who is not really a fan of Buffett's music, was visibly impressed. Jimmy Buffett is the quintessential showman, balladeer, and gentleman.

19

Out of Many

One of the things we take for granted in Jamaica is that within most of us, if we dig deep enough, is woven a tapestry of genetic surprises. The other is that the more things have changed on the surface, the more they have managed to remain the same beneath. Independence brought us legal and political freedom from England but perhaps not from ourselves. Within the parameters of my story lie all these surprises; all the difference and yet the sameness of our island. And while the realities of two Jamaicas were more obvious in colonial days, the vestiges of them remain in place to some extent even today, though now more subtle.

On this journey back through the past, I've discovered that within my blood there are traces of the Battle of Hastings, a Scottish clan, the *Mayflower*, the Battle of Saratoga, the Portuguese Jewish diaspora, and slaves from Western Africa. I don't have to do a DNA test to find this out. I only have to consider the backgrounds of the various members of my family. And I am not extraordinary. In Jamaica many families bear these combinations and contradictions.

I always knew this in the unconsidered way one grows up knowing things. But it has come home to me vividly as I have tried to piece together my family's story one which, given my personality, makes me more open than most people.

I recently visited my first cousin Pamela Melville McGregor in Brampton, a suburb not far from my Toronto home. It would prove to be a visit that would bring a whole new layer of richness to my quest to better understand my family history. Carole, myself, Rachel, and her husband Iz, picked Pamela up at her apartment to go for lunch. I had met her a few times in Jamaica many years before when her father had brought her to my business place. I knew her father, Vincent, quite well; he was one of the children of Harold's 'outside' family with Josephine Silvera. And Vincent's son, Ralston, Pam's brother, used to work for me. As I've explained, when I was growing up, outside children were usually treated in Jamaica with contempt by the 'legitimate' ones; the outside children often felt a certain amount of shame, despite the communality of blood. I was always the rebel in my family so I was the one who had some contact with the 'outsiders' over the years, becoming quite close with my Uncle Seymour, also Pam's uncle, and I was now anxious to know what Pamela knew about my grandfather and hers, Harold 'Major' Melville.

Looking back I'd been struck by the births of the Major's children – all of them. During his marriage to my grandmother Berenice, he had five children: Thomas 1913, John, 1915, Alice 1917, Douglas 1918, and Mary 1923. In his outside relationship with Josephine Silvera, he had three more sons. The first, Keith, was born in 1913; then came Vincent, in 1915; and Seymour was born in 1920. So my Uncle Tom and Keith were born in the same year, and my father and Vincent also shared the same year of birth.

It was clear to me that Major had two families going concurrently during his marriage to my grandmother, and looking at the dates, he would have to have known Josephine Silvera, probably an outside child of one of the Silveras, by the time he met Berenice, for all the Silvera clan in St Mary were related and they all grew up around the Crescent Estate, the Major's family home. Major's mother was a Silvera, so Harold and Josephine were probably distant cousins and would have known each other for years.

As Pam came down the steps of her apartment building, an elderly figure walking with the help of a cane, I was immediately overwhelmed by the contradictory strength of her personality. She reminded me of a latter day Miss Lou, Jamaica's iconic and beloved folklorist, linguist, poet and teacher from colonial and early post-colonial days – hearty, funny, irreverent, speaking in that old time Jamaica dialect with its own special words, its musical intonation, its teasing, funny associations and observations. Hers was a language of survival completely unlike the modern day Jamaican yardie-gangsta-speak that breathes anger and hardness, the victimized voice of modern day Jamaican youth. Like Miss Lou, my cousin exuded the timeless resilience, strength, and humour of the Jamaican personality throughout its history.

Today, Jamaican patois is the most sought-after creole language on the planet. The language is mimicked all over international media, on the news, in films and TV shows, and in music. Visitors to Jamaica want to learn how to speak our patois; they identify with it and speak it proudly. But it wasn't always so. The British teachers turned their noses up at our language and grammar, and teachers well-meaningly tried to stamp out its use in our schools. In the early days of our tourism, Jamaicans who worked in the industry imitated the American visitors, speaking with an 'American twang', maybe embarrassed by their own dialect. But could anyone blame them? We grew up believing everything 'foreign' was better than anything Jamaican, and that meant our patois also. Three hundred years of colonial rule has its consequences.

Pamela suggested a delightful Jamaican restaurant, King Patty House, in a strip mall whose menu featured all the old favourites – escoveitch fish, jerk chicken and pork, oxtail, mackerel run-down, fried ripe plantain and ackee and salt fish, all in huge portions that we'd wash down with kola champagne. "You okay with this?" she asked sternly, as we all emerged from the car. We were more than okay with this.

Pam and I went to the counter to order our food, oxtail for Carole and me, jerk chicken for Pam and Iz, and ackee and salt fish for Rachel, while the others hovered near a larger table further away by the door, the only one around which we could spread out in comfort and speak with some privacy. Three patrons at that table were preparing to leave. "I hope you don't mind us waiting here to push you out," Rachel joked to them.

A tall white man with a broken accent of some European descent shrugged, saying with bright-eyed pride as though it was the key to the Kingdom whose food he had eaten, "No problem". 'No problem' has become a facile universal pass-phrase for the secret of what the world believes is our island's personality and consciousness. It had the ease of Miss Lou's bantering and of Pamela's breezy personality that defiantly shrugs off an old history of suffering and injustice, offering the outsider the simple comfort of a happy destination with great music, white sand beaches, spicy food – a culture unthreatening to the visitor's conscience. It reflects nothing of the complicated social truths that we coped with in the Jamaica of yesterday and which continue to haunt us today.

We took possession of our table, opening up our styrofoam boxes, unwrapping our paper napkins to retrieve the plastic forks, and with Pamela's permission I placed the cell phone in front of her and hit the record button. She looked at it with suspicion for a moment and then seemed to forget about it. I had a list of questions I had brought with me, but which I never got a chance to take out of my pocket.

We were starving. It had been a long drive, and the lunch was there for us to pounce on. Until that is, we met Pamela's stern stare. So, the two atheists, a Buddhist, and a Jew sat quietly as Pamela thanked the Lord for the food, for bringing her cousin to her, for the mysteries of the Lord's way, the blessings that would rain on all of us if only we placed our trust and faith in Jesus Christ, forever, Amen. And as she recited all this, the tiny restaurant went silent, as though everyone else there wanted to share in the blessing. I am always amazed by the dutiful way in which even the most disenfranchised congregant in Jamaica remains faithful to God.

The Lord taken care of, Pamela took over the conversation, immediately launching into the subject of the family. It began like a roll call of the dead: Keith, her father Vincent, and Seymour had now died. She said with off-hand fatalism that her two sons, security guards, had been shot and killed in Jamaica. Her daughter Sophia who lives in New Jersey, had married a cop and they have their own restaurant. She has a grandchild she goes to see, and like all grandmothers her face lit up as she shared this. Her brother Ralston died in a car crash. This I remembered. "I dream mi bredda ded. Mi tell Mama say mi head hurting me where in de dream him was hit in the head. 'You bredda dead,' she say." And Pam roared with laughter: "'Im hit him head and him bleed to death."

I knew Ralston was a crazy driver and that the car had spun out of control and landed upside down in a ditch in the marshland on the left of the highway that leads to Kingston, and that all in the car had drowned. I have no idea whether Ralston did indeed hit his head, this version justifying Pamela's dream.

She told us how her father Vincent had helped his brother, her uncle Keith, to go to England. He had paid the fare. "So when me need help, me ask Keith to send money to help me buy books. An' im send me Football Pools coupons! Me Daddy cuss, 'im cuss 'im cuss." We looked at each other and laughed. This was so bizarre!

But when Keith came back all seems to have been forgiven, for they built a fishing boat together. They were called the 'Tarzan brothers,' she said. I think they all had the same nickname. "But they all go to work at Reynolds at one time or odder and they sell the boat and Keith move to Seaford Town where him dead." This without any emotion. "Dey held the funeral in MoBay. 'Im a big, big man and dey nearly drop he coffin!" That was apparently the end of Keith, and she brushed off her hands and moved smoothly on to the memorial service of my own father, where one of his friends had been handing out the programmes. "One hand and a hook! Me daughter nearly ded of fright. I laughed so hard! She cried."

Dad had left Jamaica in 1974 and died in Canada in December 1992. I had rushed up for the funeral, and I organized a memorial service for him in Ocho Rios on February 1, 1993, as many of the older villagers from Epworth wanted to pay their respects, and of course family and friends were there. I don't remember any friend of Dad with a hook, so I wondered if it was one of the church wardens. But I didn't call her on it; it was such a good story!

Her divorce slid by with a few more quips: "Had to lie, turn mi face. Lose him and let 'im go."

I was anxious to get a few more relevant facts – well, relevant to me now. "Was Vincent in touch with the Major?" I inquired. "Oh yes," she said. "Was he a good father?" asked Rachel, forever the nosy, sentimental one with all her personal questions.

"I think so," she said blinking for a moment as though temporarily lost outside either her story routine, her own reverie of memory, or her comfort zone. "Daddy always talk 'bout him and when he was having kids and not working. Grandpa had a property on Maxfield Avenue and Hagley Park Road." *Grandpa*, she had said. So personal and touching. It struck me how I had no name for my grandfather other than The Major. Major was good to Vin, she said, when he had kids that needed sustenance from his property: "...he need to have milk and dem something de from his father."

Courtville was one of the homes my father grew up in with his mother, my grandmother. My father as a boy flashed through my mind in an improbable picture of him indoors while outside were Keith, Vincent, and Seymour, a sort of lateral *Upstairs/Downstairs* in which the classes had been separated not only by financial station, but by the question of legitimacy. Just as in England, Jamaica's laws and the attitude of society ensured the security of the married. That licence entitled the wife and the children to not only the legacy and money of the father, but the safeguards and privileges of the state and most of all acceptance in Jamaican society. And the 'lock' of wedlock created the illusion of difference – psychological, social, and virtual – between those within its vows and those beyond it. Thus half-brothers and half-sisters grew up without the natural family benefits of knowing each other.

Pamela then set off on another riff of her dreams. "Mi never know mi grandfather, but mi dream mi see him. 'Im sit down at de dining table an' 'im was so big dat 'im two ass hang over di chair! An mi see him – a get mi get-up fi go pee pee and see. Me look 'pon him an him smile – and mi pee pee an go back ah mi bed lie down.

Vin laugh when I tell im. Seh it was mi Grandpa mi see in de dream. Dat your Grandpa – the Major!" She looked at me and we were held together in that moment by the certainty of a connection one couldn't halve with a word. We all laughed. Even in a dream Major loomed large.

"We was livin' at Crescent Lane. Daddy used to tek us to TBC to see you people," she said, suddenly forwarding her story by two generations. Tropical Battery Company, TBC, had been my company where Vincent's son Ralston worked as a branch manager. Her memory was sliding in and out of eras and times and places, from Crescent where the three sons of her grandmother, Josephine Silvera, were born, now dipping forward to the Tropical Battery Company in the late 1970s.

You people. There it was. The instinctive divide. Her use of 'you people' to describe me was as striking to me as her 'mi grandfather' for the Major. She regarded us as outside her family. We were the other, not the other way around. Good for her. "Two days before coming to Canada me see mi grandmother in a dream – she was a tall, good lookin' woman. Mi madda was short," she mused, then returned to Josephine: "She had ackee pattern on her skirt."

Then a dream about anointing Vincent's foot; apparently, he took his socks off only when he went to bathe. I remember that Vincent had very high arches and insteps like most of the Melvilles; some family members including myself suffered from *Charcot-Marie-Tooth Syndrome,* an inherited neurological disorder characterized by progressive loss of muscle tissue. No question Vincent was my uncle!

"You have more uncles you know!" I laughed and shook my head. Nothing about the Major surprised me anymore. She proceeded to tell me about Josephine having a fourth child that was found dead in a cellar with something wrapped around his neck. But this was apparently not the only extra brother she referred to. She then mentioned a paternity suit against the Major and some other pregnancy.

"Another brother lives at Six Mile Bull Bay." Pam said she had met him. "Major screw wid one of the maids. He younger than Vincent." She then proceeded to try to count all the children, including my branch of the family. "He knew all the children," she said, and mentioned some cousin Major had slept with: "Play with her and she breed. Cousin boil good soup," she concluded raucously, evoking one of Jamaica's dictionary of amusing and vulgar sayings, this one referring to intimacy between cousins.

By now her plate of chicken with rice and peas had gone cold as she only occasionally stopped long enough to eat a mouthful. I took the moment to check that the cell phone was still recording. She chewed slowly on a drumstick, holding it daintily in front of her mouth as she waited to swallow. I was struck by the thinness of her wrists and her small, beautiful hands, which remained resiliently young and graceful. I had finished my food and Carole picked up our empty styrofoam boxes and carried them off to the counter. Pamela returned a drumstick to her box, which she closed, and since she had barely eaten anything, kept it to take home.

"Had a jerk pork stand at Six Mile – can't remember his name but he has about six kids." She was referring to yet another outside son of the Major. She stroked the surface of the box thoughtfully before concluding delightedly, "Major a Ginal!" Indeed, I said, and we all shook our heads and laughed at what seemed like a moot point as it was clear by now that Major was very much a charlatan.

"Keith and Major used to kick off. Major was a tough son of a bitch. Never suffer fools gladly. Used to say if you mek your bed hard yu haffe lie down in it. Vin used to say the same thing too." She then pointed out the two years in which Major had sired sons with both Berenice and Josephine. "Heh heh – 'im a play wid everybody!"

We were ready to go, but Pamela continued her spiel. "I know Major a glutton, he die of diabetes." She described how Vincent went to a cookout the Major hosted and witnessed the Major eat calf, suckling pig, and chicken – "Ate it all! And he was stinking rich according to Vincent! We used to think he was married to a movie star." Vincent may have told Pam that Major was "stinking rich," but though Major did have a lot of property it was Berenice who was the heiress with the fortune. "Vincent say she stuck up. Never talk. Is like, 'Oh, I married to your Dad.'" The menace of that word 'married.' There it is, I thought. So Berenice knew about Keith and Vincent and Seymour. I'd always wondered. That unsympathetic confidence portrayed by my grandmother: part of me wondered how she endured all this. On the other hand, she was safe in the great house so to speak, her position ensured by her wealth, her status as a wife and white American. All the cards were stacked in her favour. And here was Pamela, a descendant of Major as surely as I was, making the best of a life that fate had compromised.

We decided to go to a nearby Tim Horton's to have coffee and keep the conversation going. Pamela then turned her ramble to Seymour, her younger uncle. "We used to call him Buck because he had the big Melville forehead. All Melville have big forehead," she said observing mine, which though not the largest of the clan was characteristically large as well.

Then she offered a thumbnail sketch of Seymour's wife. "Seymour's first wife Thelma a browning – she had pulp-out eye. Thick lens glasses. Bulge like fish. Seymour never divorce Thelma. She used to blackmail him and 'im would come ah yard and pass over the envelope with the money. Vin would ask him why he don't divorce her and Seymour say because they would find out he commit bigamy! She could have gone to court. Thelma had a man. Seymour tell her she was a bitch."

"Josephine leave her children young. She married again." She said this quite blithely as though she had been married before to the Major. "To a man in England. She had three more sons." She apparently fled to the United States after "the daddy dead and 'he' wanted everything." If he was dead what did it matter, but then I wasn't sure who 'he' was and thought better than to inquire for we were approaching rush hour and had the traffic yet to fight to get back to town.

"When Daddy had us, Uncle Keith write to Josephine to tell her dat Vin have pickney with a black woman. Mi madda neber did black, jus a likka darker than Dad. So Josephine wrote Vin and asked to see Monkey pickney dem dat 'im have. Vin burn the four corners of the letter an' send it back." An ominous act.

Though she said she didn't eat sugar – she has diabetes – Pamela stirred the cup of double-double coffee she had eagerly requested and that Carole placed in front of her, and was persuaded by Rachel to tuck into two tiny but hearty 'Tim Bits'. The bravado of her black humour that had us giggling before in King Patty House now seemed out of place in the bland aura of Tim Horton's. Her stories now seemed more like a performance. She hadn't stopped entertaining us, and looking back I realize this was probably her defence mechanism against this unfamiliar branch of the family, the unfamiliar face of her Jamaica. And I could tell she was getting tired.

"Vin cuss Keith. Keith considered himself a white man. Mary, Keith's wife, was a mawger white gal from Seaford Town. Long hair." Seaford Town whites were of German descent and carried their own stigma because rather than mix with blacks, the Germans intermarried. This didn't necessarily make them 'mawger' – skinny – but it did ensure they remained white.

"It was Josephine's mother who bring up the three boys after Josephine gone. And is mi fada bring up Keith's sons, Keith and Lloyd, after Keith gone to England." She sighed but made no value judgement on the desertion of the children by Josephine. I suppose it was commonly accepted that women left their children usually for grandparents to bring up as they sought money to send back from a better life abroad. "Vin was a good man. He lived to eighty-four. He used to say all him brudda dem a dawg. Cheat on dem wives. Mussi like Major!"

When we dropped her home, Carole and I went up to her small flat, cluttered but spotless, anxious to see some of her old family photographs. I hoped she might have a few of the Major. She didn't, but when she showed me the photo of Vincent I almost gasped. In the picture he looked white. Maybe I had forgotten how fair he was, or perhaps I remembered a darker man who lived in the sun. He looked just like my brother Christopher.

She then shyly pulled out two more: one of her mother, an exquisite browning with a long neck, wide aristocratic jaw and high cheekbones. A true beauty. And a little picture of herself as a little girl in her Trench Town High school uniform, her smile wide, her cute freckles on a sweet young face, eager, already smart and funny.

I had attended DeCarteret, Munro, and Jamaica Colleges, the three most prestigious Jamaican schools that were attended by the most privileged boys in the country. Pamela attended Trench Town High in one of the poorest urban areas of Jamaica. Trench Town is a depressed neighbourhood in the parish of St Andrew, which shares municipality with Kingston, the capital and largest city of

Jamaica. Trench Town is known worldwide as the birthplace of ska, rocksteady, and reggae music, as well as the home of reggae and Rastafari ambassador Bob Marley. The neighbourhood gets its name from Trench Pen, a 400-acre piece of land once used for livestock by Daniel Power Trench, an Irish immigrant of the eighteenth century. The Trench family abandoned the land in the late nineteenth century.

During the 1930s, Trench Pen was a growing squatter settlement for the rural to urban migrants. The colonial government's Central Housing Authority initiated a model township project which included housing, schools, the Ambassador theatre, a park, a health clinic, and a fire station. Approximately 200 acres of Trench Pen was used to create Trench Town. The new residences were built in clusters around a central courtyard with communal cooking and bathroom facilities, and they became the famous 'Government Yards' of Trench Town.

Among the musicians who grew up there, most notable was Bob Marley, who spent much of his youth in a 'government yard' on First Street. His songs 'Trench Town', 'Natty Dread', 'Trench Town Rock', and 'No Woman, No Cry' were inspired by his ghetto home. It was also home to Rastafari elder Mortimo 'Kumi' Planno, a famous Rasta teacher and friend of Bob. Trench Town was indeed the cradle of Jamaican popular music; to some it was the cradle of Jamaican self-realization... to others, our de-civilization.

This was the Jamaica I knew. Colour – shade by shade from lighter to darker – often determined who one was, how one was considered and judged by others. Worse than that, it determined how many looked at themselves.

Despite our different backgrounds, despite my privileged, upper-class family, it felt so comfortable being with my cousin.

Maybe it was because I had always been the rebel. But we all felt brighter for having spent time with Pamela. I would certainly keep in touch. What a crazy family I have!

As for the Major, he clearly turned Jamaica's national slogan and motto on its head. Instead of 'Out of many, one people,' the motto the Major lived by was, 'Out of one, many people.'

And here was one of Jamaica's daughters, a witness to the spirit of resilience Marley wrote and sang about. Here we were. One family. Common blood. Separated only by legitimacy, colour, class, and money. My story is the story of Jamaica.

AFTERWORD
Arlington 2019

The first time I visited Thomas Briggs's house on Medford Street in 2018, I was just a tourist at a heritage house. I saw the plot of land, the house from outside, the garage that was home to some of the inventions of the owner who made the place famous. Carole took pictures. We spoke to the present resident, proud owner, at the front door. Perhaps he needed to know our bona fides as strangers before he would open his doors to us. Even so, the exclusion had whetted my appetite.

Of course, it wasn't the first clue I had received about the family past. The visit Wally Parks paid me in 1993 that led to my reading the chapter, 'The Major,' from his sister's memoir, *Yes, My Darling Daughter*, had started me thinking about my paternal grandparents, Berenice and Harold. But nothing before its time I guess. I did nothing to follow up for twenty-five years.

When in the summer of 2018 I found myself standing in front of my great-grandfather's house in Arlington, Massachusetts, a house he built in 1889, and seeing the building at the rear of the house where he worked on the wire stitcher and other inventions, in that moment I made a decision that led to the telling of this story. I wanted to learn more about my grandmother Berenice Briggs who had died at the relatively young age of forty, seventeen years before I was born. I wanted to learn about Thomas Briggs, the successful inventor. I wanted to learn more about my American cousins, some of whom I had met as a kid, others never. And I wanted to learn the truth about my grandfather Harold Melville, someone I knew was a controversial figure. I wanted to know the history of the Melville family.

After that first visit, I began hiring researchers in Boston and in Jamaica, and contacting family members in far-flung places all over the world from Perth to Tahiti, from Geneva to Queensland, from Toronto to Sarasota. I was not prepared for the voluminous amount of work that was forthcoming from the two researchers, nor the invaluable input from the Lawrence and Melville cousins scattered across the globe. I had opened a floodgate.

I would write this book with Rachel's help. I swamped Rachel with emails containing all this research plus my own, and all the ensuing interviews that she is still trying to categorize. And in between her teaching, Rachel began to write, and pressed me to write. My quest was on, and we were off to the races!

Number 87 Medford Street is the cradle of my grandmother. Standing on the outside that first visit was almost like a metaphor for my family awareness up to date: I was a Melville – a Caribbean Melville, a Jamaican Melville who grew up in a macho society but whose view was tempered by the presence in my life of an honourable father, a family man. Though I had hardly known my grandfather Harold Melville, I felt his presence in my life, in my activities from horses to bird shooting. I felt at home in the landscape in which he and my father had grown up, and which had shaped us all. My grandmother, for her part, always felt like a myth – her legendary money some intangible safety net that had no face or human embrace, just a fact one knew one should not take for granted, but did.

Hopefully, wherever he is, Thomas Briggs would be able to see, like a satellite picture of Earth, the end result of all his labours. And not just in the elements of efficiency his work has produced in offices all over the world, but more intimately, snapshots of us, four generations of his progeny, scattered over the globe. I hope he has a sense of humour! If so, he'll never be bored up there.

Now on our second visit in the summer of 2019, exactly one year later, the four of us, Carole, Rachel, Iz, and I, arrived at the address again. The first thing we noticed was that the colour of the house had been changed to yellow. This gave it a warm feeling, which would be matched this time by the welcome we received. We had called before to make an appointment. When I rang the bell on the narrow porch, a smiling Deepto answered and held the door open for us.

After a lifetime it felt like I was finally in. The door had opened at last.

Entering from sunshine, I was vaguely aware of a wood-panelled gloom typical of the era in which it was built surrounding our greeting in the hall. It reminded me for a moment of Arthur's Seat, my old family home in Jamaica, whose casements of St Ann yakka wood (endemic to Jamaica – used for everything from ships' masts to yam sticks, and not to be confused with yukka, which is cassava) shone golden in brighter light around my youth. I asked about the wood and Deepto was quick to explain. "The trim and panelling in the front entry and staircase are oak. I believe they are mostly original to the house although there are clearly some pieces that have been refreshed or replaced to match."

Rachel ran her hands over the wallpaper in the front entry between the wood, which almost looked like patterned leather. Deepto explained that this wallpaper, also in a few other areas of the house is a stiff, embossed material. He said he was told by a town historian that it is probably a product called *Lincrusta* (or an imitation patterned after it). According to Wikipedia, the Lincrusta product was launched in England in the 1870s and started being manufactured in Connecticut in the early 1880s, so it may well be original to Briggs's time. "You will recall that the house dates to 1889," he reminded us. "Everywhere that it appears in the house, it is stained a rich dark brown, so as to look very much like dark leather." As we browsed and talked, I imagined the family retiring to their bedrooms at night, climbing these sturdy stairs.

Deepto's attractive English wife Jacquie stood by the inner door smiling, awaiting our invasion. We had been invited to tea. Deepto presented Jacquie and their two beautiful young daughters, Maya and Devi, with bright eyes and easily eager faces, unusual in this age of internet-tethered truculence from youth. A perfect family picture, and this was their home, not mine, and yet he was generously happy to share its memories with me.

They showed us into a long, somewhat narrow living room, which extended as a dining room towards the back of the house where, from the unseen kitchen beyond, tea would soon appear. The English are expert at tea, and their fare was excellent, as was the pot of tea. Beneath where we were seated, a rich, dark-patterned rug covered the lighter wooden floor; it was a handwoven item from Agra, India, woven in the Persian style. "We just purchased it during a family visit to India in early 2019," Deepto said with a quiet pride that reflected how much he valued his legacy.

We sat around the coffee table, the children on a bench in front of an electronic piano under the window of the far wall that faced the road, joining in with ripples of laughter and occasional mischievous asides as the adults shared stories about their lives – Deepto just back from a long academic trip, Jacquie proudly describing her children's achievements from creative writing and science to I think drama, but I can't now remember all. Carole and I described our recent visit to Australia where I got information from Briggs descendants and Carole had taken pictures. Iz talked about his early life in Russia, and Rachel spoke about her published non-fiction books, perhaps trying to present Deepto and Jacquie with her credentials for this major biographical project.

Deepto's children had grown up in this house and they had that aura of belonging that told you they knew every squeak of each floorboard and how to navigate them to avoid secret missions being revealed. I tried to conjure up the Briggs family eating their dinners, children doing their homework with the promise of a game of rummy or some other card game before bed. I felt watching the kids I was somehow coming back full circle.

Deepto himself had done a lot more research on Thomas Briggs, his wife Alice, and their daughters Helen and Berenice since my first visit. He handed us a few sheets of printed paper with pivotal dates of birth, marriage, death, purchase of houses, and the landmarks and milestones left behind in records for us to track down their past. There was also a sheet of paper with a printout of a letter by a child with Berenice Briggs's name mentioned. It was a letter dated June 6, 1901, to a news magazine; he'd come across it in his search. And, he produced a tiny photograph, placed in a cardboard holder, of a young woman's face. It made my heart jump, hoping this might be Berenice, but Carole, a portrait painter with the sharpest eye for resemblance, quickly brought up for comparison the old cameo of Berenice we had in her camera and ruled that out.

We will never know for sure who it was, but Rachel, determined to believe it was Berenice, wanted to know more. "I found it when resurfacing an old workbench in the garage," Deepto told us. "This, along with some other stiff cardboard movie posters were being used as padding of some sort under a thin surface board on top of the main wood for the workbench. I found these when I pried off this panel covering, which was in poor condition, in order to replace it. The posters are original first-run film posters from the local movie theatre, dating from the 1930s and 1940s. The fourth owner of the house was here from 1932 to 1956, followed by his daughter's family from 1956 to 1993."

Deepto's careful recounting displayed such fastidiousness with detail and truth. I felt lucky to have this committed caretaker of our original family home. After all, when you think about it, owning a home is a temporary thing. We may buy a home and live in it for a while, but homes outlive us and will pass from hand to hand.

"The garage has a large attic space that was filled with debris when we moved in," our host continued. "One item we found up there and saved was a large painted sign for a small shop belonging to the house's third owner, Luke Monroe [during 1908 to 1932]. He operated a shop on 106 Clinton Street in the Fanueil Hall marketplace. That part of Clinton Street no longer exists, as it was demolished in the urban renewal work in Boston in the mid-twentieth century, although the main part of Fanueil Hall is of course still around." A thoughtful man who studies the universe and takes nothing at all for granted.

Tea finished, and the kids who had been sent to do homework scampering overhead, it was time to go. We had taken up enough of the good professor's time. Rachel wanted to send her books to the family and asked for the postal address. We got up to say our farewells and leave, and Jacquie handed us their Christmas card with a lovely picture of the family of four and their address.

Standing in the entrance hall Carole took a few last photographs of us against the background of the rich panelling. "Does this house have secrets?" Rachel asked, as Iz rolled his eyes. But Deepto fielded all our questions with equal respect. He pointed to the panelled area under the stairs, right beside the front door.

"Here under the first part of the main staircase, there is a hidden crawlspace accessible through a panel that is actually a hinged entry door. We store luggage, etcetera, inside. My kids loved to use it as a hiding space when they were younger and playing with friends. There are many creaky floorboards and such scattered throughout the house – it is hard to move around quietly!"

A verandah I hadn't realized or perhaps not remembered lay beyond the small front porch looking over the pavement where the car was parked. I have a memory of the kids waving from the verandah, the simple happiness of youth and assured belonging lighting up their faces. As we waved back, I thought again of two girls long ago, Helen and Berenice.

I still think about that visit. There was my grandmother's childhood home, a home of two sisters, though further apart in age than the girls we'd just met. A home in which Berenice probably also played hide-and-seek and made good use of the crawl space beneath the stairs.

Flipping through Deepto's new lists of names and dates, house owners and town history, I paused to read that printout of a child's letter in a newsletter, "The Christian Work."

Dear Grandma:

I have no grandmother, and I would like to be one of your grandchildren.

I suppose that, like the old woman that lived in the shoe, you have so many children you don't know what to do. But perhaps you could find some nook to put me in. I am ten years old, and in the Fifth Grade at school. It is raining very hard today. Last Christmas, or Christmas before last, my friend, Berenice Briggs, and I had a box all ready to send to poor children. In it were dolls, books, pictures, toys, and many other things. But before we nailed it up, it tipped over and some of the pictures smashed and the dolls broke. We found it too late to fix up another box. So we did not send any. I am afraid I will crowd out many people if I write any longer. So will close with love.

Your new grandchild, Marjorie Gott

As she had in the Medford Street house, my grandmother felt real and near to me, mentioned here in a letter as a friend of a little girl called Marjorie Gott, preparing a care package for the poor and being disappointed by its misadventure. And the odd irony of this letter was that this little girl had lost her grandmother; and here was I reading her letter over a century later at a time when I too was in search of my grandmother, her friend Berenice.

I flipped over the card that Jacquie gave us. There was their daughter Maya's poem, "Silver Star," true to her astrophysicist father. I lingered on the last four lines;

Memories
  Of days gone by
Stars must have a lot of them,
  After living for a million years.

Where has this journey taken me? What have I learned about my family and what have I learned about me? Discovery, intrigue, and scandal are a few of the superficial words that come to mind. But at a deeper level it has been a very emotional journey into the past and into me. Perhaps I can say, for good or bad, I know myself better.

The nineteenth-century Scottish idiom 'confession is good for the soul' comes to mind; must be the Scots blood in me. The act of confession is therapeutic, and I feel comforted in baring my family's story and my own. I feel richer for knowing and trying to understand what transpired in our history, though some of it will be uncomfortable for some and painful to others. Family myths abound, and the danger of looking too closely is that some of the heroes may turn out to be villains; likewise, some of those thought to be villains may be redeemed. I think of the Major on one hand; I think of Leonard Lawrence on the other.

Berenice Briggs Melville is buried alone, an abandoned grave in the cemetery of the St Andrew Parish church in Kingston, thousands of miles from her family in Rhode Island, an outsider caught in a Jamaican drama I have pursued relentlessly in writing this book. Yet despite all that I've discovered on this journey, Berenice, my grandmother, remains my great unanswered quest – a shape in my heart without sufficient definition. She remains a figure for whom I will always search. She is a need in me, a thirst that has not been quenched.

As I leave this story, hers is the hand I can't let go.

As long as I keep searching, she is not forgotten.

The End

9 789768 286246